Henri Oguike's *Front Line*
Creative Insights

Henri Oguike's *Front Line*

Creative Insights

Lorna Sanders

Photographs by Guy Hoare

Dance Books
Alton

First published in 2004 by Dance Books Ltd,
The Old Bakery, 4 Lenten Street, Alton, Hampshire GU34 1HG
www.dancebooks.co.uk

Production by Liz Morrell & Patrick Donnelly
Printed by Latimer Trend & Company Ltd

ISBN: 1 85273 104 4

Contents

Introduction – using this book

This book is intended to provide teachers with material and information to support the study of Henri Oguike's *Front Line* (2002) as part of the AQA GCSE Performing Arts: Dance Specification. It will also be useful to those teaching dance at a range of other levels.

The tasks in section 4 aim to provide a variety of ideas, practical and theoretical, for approaching teaching and learning in respect of *Front Line*. Additional material will need to be collected and this is indicated in the text. Teacher's Notes are used to highlight specific points about the delivery of the tasks. Teachers should use their professional judgment to determine the order of a scheme of work appropriate to their individual circumstances. It should be noted that in the interests of doing justice to *Front Line* there is more information here than students will need for the GCSE written examination. Experienced teachers will of course use their own judgment but the inexperienced should refer to the *Specification* (2005/6), *The Teachers Guide* and past examination papers published by the AQA.

An overview, rather than a fully detailed history, of the background context of Contemporary Dance is given since it is likely that most teachers will be familiar with this. For ease of reference a resource list is provided for those interested in exploring this context further.

Acknowledgements

I wish to extend my heartfelt thanks to Henri Oguike, Guy Hoare and Elizabeth Baker for the generous manner in which they allowed me to interview them for this book. Also thank you to Isabel Tamen and Iyshea McKay of Henri Oguike Dance Company for providing additional information so quickly – a boon when I was writing under pressure.

Lorna Sanders MA

Fact Page: *Front Line* (2002)

Premièred as *Of Death and Stillness* (2001)

Choreographer:	Henri Oguike
Composer:	Dmitry Shostakovich
Lighting:	Henri Oguike
Costume:	Liliana Mendonca
Première:	Teatro Tivoli, Lisbon 11th May, Companhia Portuguesa de Bailado Contemporaneo [1]
Dancers:	Claudia Sampaio, Susana Lima, Rita Reis, Roberto Silva, Jann Seabra, Pedro Dias, Emilio Cervello
Acknowledgements:	Lisboa Camara Municipal and Camara Municipal Cultura, Cascais Camara Municipal, Ministerio Da Cultura, Instituto Do Emprego e Formacao Profissional, The British Council, Barriga Killer Fitness Club

Front Line (UK première 2002 - Henri Oguike Dance Company)

Choreographer:	Henri Oguike
Composer:	Dmitry Shostakovich
Lighting:	Guy Hoare
Costume:	Elizabeth Baker
Première:	31st January, British Dance Edition [2] Crescent Theatre, Birmingham
Dancers:	Nuno Campos, Charlotte Eatock, Khamlane Halsackda, Mey Lin-Chapman, Olga Nikiditis, Nuno Silva
Live Music:	the Con Tempo 4tet
Acknowledgements:	co-funded by a consortium of venues: Swindon Dance; Swan Theatre, High Wycombe; The Point, Eastleigh; The Gantry, Southhampton. Live music assisted financially by the Hattori foundation

---

[1] now called Companhia de Bailado Contemporaneo.

[2] British Dance Edition is the annual industry showcase that advertises contemporary dance for national and international promoters. Some of its performances are also open to the public.

Video (2003)

Credits

Dancers:	Nuno Campos, Nuno Silva, Charlotte Eatock, Katharine Kerr, Sarita Piotriowski, Sarah Storer.
Musicians:	Artea Quartet
Producer/Director:	Steve Jackman
Online Editor:	Simon Aeppli
Executive Producer for Arts Council England:	Jennifer McLachlan
Production:	The Place Videoworks
Acknowledgements:	Funded by Arts Council England

Part 1
The Creators

Biographies, careers and characteristics of their work

- *Choreographer: Henri Oguike*
    - *Choreochronicle*
    - *Choreographic Characteristics of Henri Oguike*

- *Composer: Dmitry Shostakovich*

- *Lighting Designer: Guy Hoare*

- *Costume Designer: Elizabeth Baker*

Henri Oguike performing the solo *F.P.S Part 1*

The Choreographer: Henri Oguike

Expanded from an article written for *Dancing Times*, March 2003, (Sanders 2003). Note: for ease of reading, unless stated otherwise, quotation of Henri Oguike is from (Oguike 2003).

Music

Henri Oguike's career is a demonstration of his continuing faith in the primacy of the relationship between music and dance. His focus on music is unusual among young chore-ographers: 'most innovative of all, by contemporary standards... is his use of music, which is usually classical and often played live' (Frater 2002, n.p.). His choices are also unusually eclectic, ranging from Piazzolla to Shostakovich and Bartok to Aubry.

Early dance experience

Henri Oguike was born in West Glamorgan, the son of a Nigerian father and Welsh mother. Introduced to dance classes by a friend, he went on to take A Level dance and drama at Swansea College. Regretting giving up music previously (he could play the recorder), he also studied music there. He had to learn to play the piano quickly for his studies thus showing a keen sense of determination.

From 1991 he attended London Contemporary Dance School and joined '4D', their postgraduate performance group in 1994 for whom he also made *Doors and Sundials*. Later that year he became a founder member of the Richard Alston Dance Company. Sympa-thetic to Alston's ideals, he joined the company to learn more. As a performer Oguike was 'eye-catching ... his dark looks paired with a scything decisiveness about his way of moving' (Brown 2002a). Of Alston, Oguike said 'you're not just purely an instrument' (Anonymous 1998). Finding something personal to respond in the work was important.

Alston was a significant influence. In speaking of Oguike and Martin Lawrence, he points out;

they both work with a coherent dance language that deals with steps and deals with detail, thus the moves are involved with music and structure and all those things to do with honing a craft. So that's great, great to see people who worked that way with me. They are not imitating. They've gone on to make their own language.

(Alston in Polzer 2004, p.23)

Oguike also expresses an interest in the work of Christopher Bruce (ex Artistic Director of Rambert Dance Company), Sir Kenneth MacMillan (ex Director and principal choreographer of the Royal Ballet) and the postmodern Belgian choreographers, Anne Teresa de Keersmaeker and Wim Vandekeybus. This indicates an unusual breadth of taste for different styles of choreography and methods of working.

Amongst Shadows (1996)

An award from the Robin Howard Foundation allowed Oguike to create *Amongst Shadows* in 1996.[3] It premièred at the Resolution season at The Place. A description of the dance is revealing: 'lighting is dim, partial ... Marinelli's score is an industrial rumble and whine ... six dancers ... are an assembly line, their hands chopping and clenching, their footsteps echoing. Occasionally one or more will scoot out of line, an arm or shoulder chipped by the light. Oguike ... suggests that the dancers only come alive amongst shadows' (Jays 1996). The interests are already clear; a strong theatrical presentation, lighting as a significant contributor, and an elusive emotional content wedded to an abstract base.

The success of *Amongst Shadows* encouraged Oguike to present his first full evening of work at the Gulbenkian Acarte Theatre, Lisbon and in 1997 he won the prestigious Jerwood Award for young choreographers. *The Brutality of Fact*, for Spring Loaded 1998 followed; in which two tightly locked dancers (Oguike and Tamen) grapple with each other, his gripping fingers pulling back her face, her imprisoning arms grasped around him in mutual combat. [4]

---

[3] Isobel Tamen, a Portuguese dancer, performed in this work. She was with the Richard Alston Company and had also been a member of London Contemporary Dance Theatre. She is now Oguike's wife and company manager.

[4] Description of a photograph in (Foley 1999).

A moment of give (1999)

In 1998 Oguike left the Richard Alston Dance Company to pursue an independent career. His plans to go to Europe were abandoned when, while tired and teaching, he snapped an Achilles tendon. He used the recovery period for contemplation instead. In 1999 he was commissioned by the Acarte Theatre to create *Prime Origin* and in September he made *A moment of give* for the Studio Theatre, London. Company information lists this latter work as

> an emotionally charged quartet to the music of Shostakovich. Four women console each other through fear, anger and frustration in the aftermath of loss. Using the music as the primary influence, the dance echoes its ethereal, taut and humorous aspects.

(Anonymous 2002b)

Mackrell notes how in Shostakovich's Second Piano Trio, played live on stage, 'machine rhythms grind beneath echoes of an older folk tradition, and it's this sense of danger that animates Oguike's choreography'(Mackrell 2001). Originality was displayed: in the use of simple steps, 'runs, walks, little jumps, a thrust of weight to right or left, an upward push of the arms'(Percival 2001); frequent and compelling contrasts between motion and stillness; and the implied relationships inherent within the dance.

Henri Oguike Dance Company

The success of *A moment of give* prompted the founding of the Henri Oguike Dance Company, because it 'was the most positive way to move forwards'. They were well received and given a *Time Out* Live Award for the Most Outstanding New Company in 2001.

Doris Humphrey and rhythm

Music, and particularly its rhythmic content, is the base of Oguike's work. It is not used for mere slavish interpretation. *Front Line* (2002) is evidence of what he wrings from it; 'the dancers wear ... fierce expressions, clenching fists, slapping each other's bodies, making sudden jumps with slashing feet, and keeping a stamping rhythm going with their bare feet like a drum-roll announcing the end of time ... I was lost in admiration when he turned a four-part fugue in the music into a six-part fugue in the dance' (Brown 2002a). Oguike acknowledges Doris Humphrey as a source of interest. Humphrey writes: 'of all the ingredients in the art of the dance, rhythm is the most persuasive and most powerful element ... but is also one of the least used' (1959, p.104).

Melancholy Thoughts (2001)

Music also provides 'ideas to realise. I search the music and put the boundaries in myself. For example, we took the idea of the ground being very hot in *Melancholy Thoughts*. Other dynamics can then start to creep in. I begin by visualising clearly though it makes less sense for me now to fully furnish the movement on my own body'. Oguike's work requires a strong input from his dancers. Rather than a mechanical learning of steps, he stresses motivation as vital (as does Humphrey). He explains that this may be motional, such as 'getting the rhythm in the legs and then seeing how the quality on the top of the body might be affected by this'. Or it may be emotional. In *Melancholy Thoughts* 'a man raises his curved arm - an invitation for a woman to join him, yet threatening. The women flick their bare legs out erotically, but they also rumble their heels on the ground' (Brown 2002b).

Shot Flow (2001)

Improvisation, as a tool, becomes increasingly important and more specifically, a method Oguike calls *points work*. This began with *Shot Flow* and he continues to explore its potential. He explains; 'for example, take four points in space, [he draws a simple square shape in the air] these can become points on the body, surfaces or joints to be connected in someway, you can work inside of the shape, or outside it, or you can connect point to point, by direct or indirect means, etc'. Oguike clearly enjoys collaborating with dancers; 'finding something genuinely for themselves, the process itself is interesting'.

Interest in lighting

Shot Flow demonstrates another interest, being 'notable for its imaginative use of light as a full partner in the choreography' (Craine 2002a). Guy Hoare is his collaborator in this. Lighting has played an increasingly significant role in establishing territory, enhancing mood, and conjuring drama. During *In broken tendrils* (2002), for example, the green light suddenly transforms the ground into a grassy expanse …a circular spot picks out a man occupied in violent undulations and corkscrews… another horizontal beam, flickering like a strobe, converts a spinning dancer into a jerky human spool.

(Craine 2002b)

Dido & Aeneas (2003)

Oguike tackled a more plot-driven project than usual, making a selection of music from Purcell's *Dido & Aeneas* with the objective of creating a small, intimate piece. An initial concept of a board game with the gods looking down was simplified to the idea of the characters being pieces in a game. (Something of the original notion was evident when Sarah Storer who danced both Dido and the Sorceress, with lowered head, out flung arms and an audible expelling of breath, suddenly brought the other dancers to life.) Oguike researched the characteristics of the era of the music to help set a style, for example, 'in the way that the weight drops into one hip when people are at ease. Posture is significant. We explored four ways of dancing: intimate, personal, social, public. Is it possible to mix these attitudes, a 'public' focus for the head with an 'intimate', closed torso for example?' The body thus becomes dual, coded and ambiguous; the use of the torso expressive not just functional or decorative. This is a characteristic in general.

Oguike and Hoare talked about 'the space, the concept, the music, the movement in order to hone in on some abstraction of ideas'. Dido treads solemnly along a narrow track of light that bisects the stage like a tightrope; a striking metaphor for her fate. Later, on a darkened stage, she is caught in a lonely glow of light for a breathless, spiky, broken-limbed descent to the floor as she dies of a broken heart. This illustrates how lighting adds to the drama and also how Oguike makes striking visual images from quite basic gestural vocabulary. Mackrell writing of a later piece (*White Space*) points to a key issue in general, that Oguike's work involves an unusual and 'careful balance between representation and abstraction' (Mackrell 2004). Not many contemporary dance choreographers work closely with narrative and music quite in this way, Kim Bandstrup and Mark Morris are two who spring readily to mind.[5]

Oguike remains committed to performing with live music wherever possible (rare for a

---

[5] Mark Morris made his own version of Dido & Aeneas in 1989 and dances the dual role of Dido and Sorceress himself.

small company) and expresses an ambitious wish that he could afford to work intensively with musicians over time as he does with Hoare. He is not short of big ideas and has the clear objective of developing his company in every way possible. In 2002 an Easter course for young people at the Studio Theatre, Westminster, led to the founding of a sister youth dance company, H20, to forge stronger links between the main company and its education work. He feels that education, in general, is an underdeveloped area and that there is a need 'to find a balance between technique and some other reason why it is important ...to get people to understand something'.

Eclectic approach

His eclectic interests, wedded to an analytical and thoughtful approach to music, have resulted in an unusually large choreographic palette; 'you simply don't see contemporary dance-makers whcan use specific subtleties of hand gesture as well as big, whole-body dives, or zen-like stillness as well as forceful momentum ... high jiving lifts and swift jumps as well as ... lyrical arabesques' (Brown 2002b). Oguike is also interested in a notion of 'tight and loose energy and how it would flow, the contrast between stillness and action and how they prepare for and service each other'. This is particularly evident in his own solo, the reworked *F.P.S* (*frames per second*) originally made in 2002 for the First Class Air Male programme. Oguike felt that experimenting with lighting had been time-consuming and neglected the musical aspect somewhat. He wanted to refocus on this. The Kronos Quartet provided new music, *Peace Piece* by Bill Evans. A contemplative dance with subtly textured, idiosyncratic gestures is the result; he drops like a praying mantis, limbs settle and rebound, sharpness suddenly diminishes into soft focus, disjointed actions softly ricochet and draw attention to enigmatic articulations. The title refers to film terminology, the speed at which individual frames are shown (25 frames creating a smooth rather than a jerky projection).

Finale (2003)

Finale, to music by René Aubry, is more than a crowd pleaser; though it certainly is that. Dancers cascade up and down the stage, brimming over in carnival mood. Movement spills out of them; costumes in terracotta colours echo the earthy qualities of the terre-à-terre footwork and swivelling hips. Oguike wanted to deal specifically with rhythm and show off the dancers' abilities. He responded to the different musical colours by varying shape and pattern in the dance. Section 1 used an idea of a square dance: 'a tight knit, simple structure contained within a small square of space and I'm working with a canonic idea here. It is in 4/4 and with an 8 bar change so I can introduce shifts, drawing from the music, like adding an extra line to it visually in order to appreciate the music visually a little more'. Although certainly no clone of Alston it is here that he sounds most like him.

Variety

Oguike's work shows unusual variety. His range of musical choices challenges him to this and he also tries to provide a balanced programme for his company. Of the 2002 tour, Meisner notes, 'he shows a rich imagination that pulls his creativity in all directions to produce widely divergent pieces' (Meisner 2002, n.p.). He is of course also in the early stages of his career and one feels that he does not yet want to be pinned down. In 2003 he stated that he was 'still in the sorting out period'. He is remarkably organised in terms of his long term thinking and the choice of sometimes quite difficult music and exploration into more overt narrative shows that he is more than willing to take risks. This is not only true of the 2002 tour (quoted by Meisner above) it is equally true of 2003 and 2004. *White Space* (2004) is set to harpsichord music by Scarlatti and introduces the use of a back projection.

> Performed with a peacock precision against a moving Mondrian-style grid, both stage and screen had a wonderful zing. Seven white-clad dancers strut with electric clarity... a flurry of moves ... extend and disrupt formality. There's an exaggerated courtly swoon, a bow that seems close to retching, savagely pecking wrists ... this is a musically voracious choreographer in confident form.
>
> (Jays 2004, p.37)

New challenges

In May 2005 Oguike creates his first site specific work in the cathedral at Bury St Edmonds, in collaboration with the Britten Symphonia. He explains his interest is 'in how dancers and musicians might communicate across a larger space than normal', how to keep things flexible enough to respond to the space itself and the possibilities of only partially revealing the dancers (Oguike 2004). Hoare is hoping to shine light in from outside the stained glass windows. Oguike is also working on a major refurbishment of *Seen of Angels* (2000), the first piece he made for the Companhia Portuguesa de Bailado Contemporaneo, Lisbon. He was interested in working with chiaroscuro, dark and light contrasts. There was a section with side lights from one direction only, so that the dancers masked their own or each other's bodies by throwing intense shadows. But in 2000 there were tight time constraints and he was travelling back and forth between the UK and Portugal. He is thus revisiting these ideas with his own company. In addition to his usual *points work* approach he is exploring *framing* as a method for evolving body design. For example, a gesture directly in front of the torso can be shifted to the side and placed in an imaginary frame against the background. This promotes a frieze-like relationship between the torso and limbs when a frontally organised torso pulls against the direction of the gesture to produce a tension between the two. The frame can also be scaled down or increased, allowing the size and context of the body part in relationship to the torso to be explored.

Oguike is an award winning choreographer however he still wants to continue performing for the time being; 'there is always something more you can be learning from performance'.[6]

---

[6] Awards: three Robin Howard Foundation awards; a Jerwood award; a *Time Out* Live award for Most Outstanding New Company in 2001; finalist in the Best Choreography category in the Critics Circle National Dance Awards in 2002, nominated for Outstanding Repertoire for the Critics Circle National Dance Awards in 2003; and finalist in the TMA Theatre Awards in the Outstanding Achievement in Dance category, 2004.

Choreochronicle of Henri Oguike

Source: Henri Oguike Dance Company and author's personal archive.
(Abbreviation: HODC: Henri Oguike Dance Company. m., music; l., lighting; c., costume)

Date	Title	Music/design/lighting	Company/notes
1994	*Doors and Sundials*		4D (London Contemporary Dance School postgraduate performance group)
1996	*Pulse*		Harrison Birtwistle Educational Project, with musicians from London Sinfonietta.
	Amongst Shadows	m. Dario Marinelli	Created with award from the Robin Howard Foundation, Resolution 96! Season, The Place Theatre, London. Remounted for 4D.
	Spool of Threads	c. Elizabeth Baker	Created with award from the Robin Howard Foundation. Part of programme of work at Acarte Theatre, Lisbon.
	Sketches to Portraits		London Contemporary Dance School for graduate students
1998	*The Brutality of Fact*		Created with an award from the Jerwood Foundation. Duet for Oguike and Isabel Tamen.
	Prime Origin	(l. Guy Hoare from 2000)	Acarte Theatre, Lisbon, 'The Body to Body' Festival. Reworked for HODC, premièred at Studio Theatre, London, 1999.
	Train (*Ride to the Abyss*)		Graduate students of Lewisham College.
	Ile aye	m. Caetano Veloso; c. Elizabeth Baker (l. Guy Hoare from 2000)	Intoto Dance (London Studio Centre performance group). Reworked for HODC, premièred at Studio Theatre, London, Autumn 1999.[7]

[7] A company advertising leaflet for the Spring 2002 tour gives the première as Spring 2000, Weymouth College. HODC listing gives Studio Theatre, London 1999. The former was the first UK tour with new lighting, the later a launching platform for the company.

1999	*A moment of give*	m: Shostakovich; c. Elizabeth Baker; (l. Guy Hoare from 2000)	Commissioned by Studio Theatre, North Westminster, London. Premièred at Studio Theatre, London, Autumn.
2000	*Seen of Angels*		Companhia Portuguesa de Bailado Contemporaneo, Lisbon. Reworked for HODC 2004.
	Language		Commissioned by Escola Superior de Danca, Lisbon
	Play To Win		Commissioned by Soho Theatre and co-produced with Yellow Earth Theatre.
	Travel Matrix		Commissioned by UK Rocks National Tour.
2001	*Apollo New Apollo*		Commissioned by Dance East. Henri Oguike and composer John Cooney exploring starting points based on Stravinsky's ballet score Apollo
	Shot Flow	m. Pedro Carneiro; l. Guy Hoare; c. Elizabeth Baker	Duet for HODC. Premièred at Studio Theatre, London, Spring.
	Of Death And Stillness	m. Shostakovich; l. Henri Oguike c. Liliana Mendonca	Companhia Portuguesa de Bailado Contemporaneo, Lisbon. Remounted as *Front Line* in 2002 for HODC.
	White Space	m. Scarlatti; c. Elizabeth Baker; l. Guy Hoare	Companhia Portuguesa de Bailado Contemporaneo, Lisbon. Premièred by HODC at Wyvern Theatre, Swindon, January 2004. Also part of British Dance Edition 2004.
	La, la, la...		National Youth Dance Company
	Melancholy Thoughts	m. Piazzolla, c. Elizabeth Baker; l. Guy Hoare	For HODC. Premièred at Studio Theatre, London in the Spring.
	Casual Grace		Bare Bones Dance Company
2002	*Bright Side*		Transitions Dance Company
	Broken Strings		Swindon National Youth
	F.P.S. *(Frames Per Second)*	2002 : m. Schubert; l. Guy Hoare.	For First Class Air Male Tour and DanceEast. Premièred Norwich

		2003: m. Bill Evans, played by Kronos Quartet.	Playhouse, May. Reworked 2003 with new music. Solo for Henri Oguike.
	Violet		Commissioned by the Curve Foundation
	Butterfly Grid	c. Elizabeth Baker	London Contemporary Dance School graduate students
	Front Line	m. Shostakovich; c. Elizabeth Baker; l. Guy Hoare	Rework of *Of Death and Stillness*. Premièred by HODC at British Dance Edition, January.
	In broken tendrils	m. Bartok; l. Guy Hoare; c. Elizabeth Baker	Premièred by HODC at The Point, Eastleigh, Spring.
2003	*Finale*	m: Rene Aubry; c. Elizabeth Baker; l. Guy Hoare	Premièred at South Hill Park Arts Centre, Bracknell, January .
	Dido & Aeneas	m. Purcell; c. Elizabeth Baker; l. Guy Hoare	Premièred at the South Hill Park Arts Centre, January
	With My Sighs		West Glamorgan Youth Dance Company.
	Splinter	m. Peteris Vasks; c. Kasumi Morimura	Laban Centre graduate students.
	Duet		For Escapade on the South Bank, commissioned by kademi/South Asian Dance UK
2004	*Signal*	m. Japanese taiko drumming; c. Elizabeth Baker	Phoenix Dance Theatre
	Parade	m. kodo drumming and Tunisian lute	London Contemporary Dance School graduate student
	F.P.S (Frames Per Second) Part 2	c. Elizabeth Baker; l. Guy Hoare	Premièred by HODC, Wyvern Theatre, Swindon, January. Shown with *F.P.S. Part 1*.
	Spatial Signatures	l. Guy Hoare	National Youth Dance Wales
2005	*Seen of Angels*	c. Elizabeth Baker; l. Guy Hoare	Reworked from 2000 (Companhia Portuguesa de Bailado Contemporaneo, Lisbon).

Choreographic Characteristics of Henri Oguike

- Music as the key starting point (frequent use of classical composers)

- Music visualisation, counterpoint and non pulse-based breath rhythm[8]

- Rhythmical emphasis in feet and legs

- Complex use of feet and parts of feet: flexed, stretched and relaxed

- Wide ranging eclectic vocabulary includes recognisable dance steps and pedestrian actions

- Striking and evocative visual images

- Use of stillness and frieze forms

- Interest in energy flow (tight and loose) and contrasts between motion and stillness

- Dynamic range is usually linked to music

- Complex use of torso: Cunningham influenced, off-kilter; allowed to be affected by leg or arm gestures; functional, decorative and expressive uses

- Spatial aspects (sometimes linked to lighting design) can determine vocabulary at times

- Linear pathways are a strong feature

- Formalist treatment usually, with elusive and emotional narrative elements

- Ensemble interest: canon, unison, contrast, complementing; formal relationships and spatial arrangements; sometimes sets a soloist or small group against the larger group

- Theatrical presentation and importance of lighting design as key part of the collaborative process

- Dancers increasingly part of the collaborative process

[8] Music Visualisation – the music determines the structure of the dance, so for example, if you turn down the sound while watching a video/DVD you still 'see' the music because the movement echoes its rhythm, phrasing, pulse, rise and fall etc. Counterpoint – the movement runs counter to the music in some way, in one sense it provides another musical line that runs in parallel with it, the dance is given an independent rhythm and crosses the musical accents or metre. Breath rhythm or non pulse-based – the dance follows its own rhythm/phrasing and is not determined by outside accompaniment.

The Composer: Dmitry Shostakovich (1906 -1975)

Early experiences

Dmitry Shostakovich lived during turbulent historical times. He was born in St Petersburg (later called Leningrad) in 1906. The year before his birth the Tsar's troops massacred demonstrators in the palace square and in 1917 the Russian Revolution broke out. This was followed by economic collapse, civil war and famine. Shostakovich, much affected by the suffering, wrote a Funeral March to the Victims of Revolution for a memorial service in 1918.[9] The Conservatoire of Music was directed by Glazunov who struggled 'to continue its tradition and teaching' (Steen 2003, p.848).[10] Shostakovich enrolled there in 1919 but life was difficult. He developed tuberculosis and needed to earn money, when his father died in 1922, by playing the piano in cinemas. These were frightening years and made a lasting impression,

> both Shostakovich's Second and Twelfth Symphonies describe the murder of a Cossak boy: and the third movement of the Twelfth is entitled 'Aurora', after the cruiser whose guns ... signalled the Winter Palace attack ... the birth of the Soviet Union.
>
> (Jackson 1997, p.28).[11]

Modernism and Russia

Immediately prior to and following the Revolution the Russian avant-garde had been developing new strands of Modernism in the arts. Russians had looked to Europe (France in particular) for cultural influences but now they became interested in their own ethnic sources. Russian Suprematism drew upon peasant styles and forms to introduce increasingly

---

[9] Shostakovich was something of a prodigy. He had begun to take piano lessons at the age of nine and by eleven he was composing.

[10] Glazunov was among the many artists who left Russia during this era, escaping to France when it became clear that he would be persecuted for his artistic beliefs.

[11] Lenin's troops attacked the Winter Palace and ousted the government in 1917.

abstract and geometric approaches in painting, and within sculpture Constructivism used factory-made materials to idealise the modern world. Diaghilev brought Russian ballet and opera to Europe. In music Rimsky-Korsakov borrowed folk elements. 'Shostakovich had the appetite and the ears to absorb everything he heard ... he flirted with Constructivism ... and the sculptor Tatlin's revolutionary spiral design became the tacit emblem of [his] own works in their raucous evocations of factory life' (Jackson 1997, p.19). The sense of optimism that was initially felt was quickly dashed as extreme forms of Marxism prevailed. State control of artists began to overthrow the Modernist avant-garde and established a new order of Russian collectivism where art served the needs of the community in a functional, accessible way. In spite of the success of his First Symphony in 1929 when he was only eighteen years old Shostakovich still had to undertake an examination in Marxist theory.

> At least there was some humour in the midst of the gloom. They were asked what was the difference, from a sociological and economic point of view, between the work of Chopin and Liszt. When he and his colleagues fell about laughing, the examination had to be adjourned until the next day.   (Steen 2003, p.849)

Initially Shostakovich was part of the Modernist movement. Constructivist principles encouraged objectivity while lyricism and harmony were abandoned. His was 'a modernism of primitive motor rhythms, unexpected turns and jumps in the melodic writing ... and a theatrical spirit of burlesque' (Ottaway 1978, p.14). Modernism was then severely repressed under Stalin's twenty-five years of brutal dictatorship (he succeeded Lenin in 1928). Stalin liquidated political enemies and established the Gulags (concentration camps) in which to imprison dissenters. Socialist Realism within the Arts was enforced as the only state-tolerated style. It supported Stalin's political regime as propaganda which sentimentalised the proletarian work ethic and idealised the new Soviet culture and its leaders.

Oppression and repression

A foretaste of how Shostakovich's work would be treated occurred in 1929 with the completion of his first opera, *The Nose*. In spite of its popular success some thought its complexity and formalism too inaccessible. Modernist decadence, as it was known, was hazardous to adhere to and perhaps 'the sense of tragedy incipient in ... Shostakovich's work was as dangerous as his experimentation' (Jackson 1997, p.34). By 1930 he was obliged to denounce his own music. In 1932 he married and was elected to the board of the Union of Soviet Composers, state approval having been earned temporarily. However, any stability in political life was impossible. With faction-fighting and intermittent purges life was never secure.

In 1930 Shostakovich started work on *Lady Macbeth of Mzensk*. Eventually cleared by the censor it premièred in 1934 and was an immediate international success. In 1936 Stalin walked out during a performance of it. He probably 'disliked ... the opera's ... desperate consecration of love above all other ties ... [and] sensed its innately counter-revolutionary individualism' (MacDonald 1999, p.3). Critics now condemned the work's Modernism. Fear of Stalin, who exerted control through terror, was uppermost. Shostakovich continued to work on his Fourth Symphony, trying to maintain artistic integrity. Stalin's rule was a cruel time in Russia: Shostakovich's sister and husband were arrested; relatives were exiled; and one of his friends executed. Eventually he was also arrested and interrogated but released, apparently almost accidentally.[12] Shostakovich cancelled the première of his Fourth Symphony in 1936, either it was too dangerous to proceed or Stalin's officials let it be known that he should request its withdrawal. The tone of tragedy in the music did not equate perhaps with Stalin's view that life was getting better (although the years 1934 - 39 comprise that period called the Great Terror, during which Stalin's zeal for repressive purges became ever more excessive).

In spite of this Shostakovich's Fifth Symphony was a success in 1937.[13] Western critics admire its abstract qualities but Russians responded to its expressive directness and

at its première they were in tears: as the last note died, the hall exploded into a forty-minute ovation ... a group of Party activists mounted the stage and proposed that a telegram of greeting should be sent to the composer from his audience.

(Jackson 1997, p.50)

There was some frightened press comment about its Western influences but Shostakovich later received a Stalin Prize for it in 1940. The dictator liked to keep his minions off balance perhaps? Shostakovich wrote his First String Quartet in 1938.

---

[12] His interrogator ordered him to reappear after the weekend but was then himself arrested so Shostakovich was sent away when he returned.

[13] He took care to subtitle it 'a Soviet artist's response to just criticism'. This may be ironical of course.

The War Symphonies

During the Second World War Shostakovich became a fire-fighter and helped to defend Leningrad during the German siege of 1941 when so many people died. Work on his Seventh Symphony began at this time. Soon he and his family were evacuated on Stalin's orders and he completed the symphony in Kubyshev. It was another international success, receiving public ovations in the UK and USA but he remained in danger from Stalin's capricious moods. His Eighth Symphony was written at the height of the war in 1943. Initially its dark tones seemed to express the horrors of this but commentators such as Dmitry Tolstoy also note a meaning that was closer to home, 'it is about totalitarianism - this horrible reality, and the pitiable human soul which is looking for a place to hide from it' (MacDonald 1999, p.6).

The Ninth Symphony was begun in the spring of 1945 after the Allied victory over German forces. At its première the conductor Evgeny Mravinsky told his players, 'I need to hear the trampling of steel-shod boots' (Jackson 1997, p.56).[14] In Russia the symphony 'is a form expected to embody some identifiable human content, if not a specific programme' (Ottaway 1978, p.9).[15] Shostakovich initially intended it as a celebratory piece, to 'express a program that [he] described as the awakening of the masses' but changed his mind (Schiavo 2003, n.p.). A friend, Isaac Glickman, recalled that Shostakovich was ambivalent about expressing too joyful a mood since 'he was afraid that on the crest of this victory, Stalin would consolidate his tyranny (MacDonald 1999, p.6). Also the horrific war had cost millions of Russian lives; 'it has long been clear that the traumas of those years had a greater impact on Shostakovich than anything else in his previous experience' (Ottaway 1978, p.33). It was to be eight years before he wrote another symphony. Partly he was interested in creating for string quartets but also his music was continually attacked by the Stalinists.

In 1944 Stalin ordered Shostakovich to work with Khatchaturian on a new national anthem and then rejected it. In 1948 one of his friends was again denounced but Shostakovich received high commendation: appointed to the Russian Supreme Soviet; awarded the Order of Lenin; and nominated as a People's Artist of Russia.

---

[14] The mood is clear whether the boots referred to are inferred as Nazi (as in the attacking German forces) or as a metaphor for Stalinist repression.

[15] Hence the criticism of modernism as being merely empty formalism.

The banning of Shostakovich's music

Suddenly, instant disgrace. The Central Committee 'condemned his ... music as formalistic and anti-democratic' (Steen 2003, p.852). During a three-day composers' Plenum his work, along with that of Prokofiev and Khatchaturian, was denounced.[16] Shostakovich issued a statement again recanting his music and perhaps saved himself from arrest. He was stripped of all official positions and his music banned from public performance by the notorious Zhdanov decree. Shostakovich was humiliated. Although there was no chance of immediate publication, he wrote a song cycle, From Jewish Folk Poetry. At this moment (following the murder, on Stalin's orders, of the Jewish actor Salmon Mikhoels) 'any identification with the Jewish community was fraught with peril' (Jackson 1997, p.61).

Re-instatement

Stalin exercised control by being unpredictable. In 1949 he sent Shostakovich, as a cultural ambassador, to take part in a conference in the USA and lifted the banning order on much of his work. This same year Shostakovich was part of the committee organising celebrations for Stalin's 70th birthday (he would have had no choice). Shostakovich appears to have made sure that any published compositions were politically correct but it seems he continued to write more substantial music in secret. In 1950 he was allowed to visit Leipzig to mark the 200th anniversary of the death of J.S. Bach and in 1951 he was re-elected to the Supreme Soviet. Even then his work was still condemned as tainted with modernism and as being not Russian enough. After Stalin's death in 1953 conditions improved but his Tenth Symphony was still criticised, some declaring it 'not "realistic", too pessimistic, and not at all representative of Soviet life; [while] others praised its assertion of creative freedom' (Grout and Palisca 1996, p.703).

The long shadow of Stalin

In 1956 in spite of there being a new Soviet leader (Krushchev) *Lady Macbeth* was still banned. Shostakovich turned increasingly to writing some very personal string quartets. His

---

[16] Stalin would have had to agree to this and may even have instigated it.

Seventh String Quartet, written in 1960 was dedicated to his first wife, Nina, who had died in 1954. Eventually a measure of freedom returned. By 1961 he was emboldened to use poems which condemned anti-Semitism but this still proved too controversial. Shostakovich, although partly a victim of Stalin, was also seen by some to be complicit with him and his position continued to be controversial. Many felt it was not clear how much his professed support of the Soviet regime was actually heartfelt or how much he merely paid it lip-service in order to survive. In spite of his modernising tendencies he appears to have denounced others who tried to stand up for greater freedom and his reputation was compromised in the West too for a time.[17]

Obituary and legacy

Shostakovich died in 1975 having written his last string quartet, the Fifteenth, less than a year before. He has at different times been described 'as a genius, a victim of the pressures of Soviet society, an heroic figure or lackey of the regime' (Ottaway 1978, p.7). His obituary in *Pravda* cited him 'a faithful son of the Communist party ... who devoted his entire life to reaffirming ... the ideals of Socialist humanism and Internationalism' (Jackson 1997, p.15). He received numerous honours during his life (several Stalin Prizes and the Order of Lenin). Four years after his death a music journalist, Solomon Volkov, escaped from Russia (which was still behind the Iron Curtain) and published *Testimony* claiming it to be Shostakovich's biography. In it Shostakovich appears to reject the politics of the Soviet era. Claim and counterclaim over its authenticity make it difficult to determine if it contains Shostakovich's memoirs or not. Some have stated that his symphonies are coded criticisms of the regime and that the book reflects views that he could not have safely expressed before. They assert that in Shostakovich's music there is the sound of

> the solitary game of an oppressed and unhappy man ... you hear insect stridulations that seem to inhabit the same worlds as Bartók or Schoenberg; but they frame scenes of desolation which make their dispassion all the more sinister. The musical doodlings with which the Eighth or the Fifteenth Symphonies die away ... hint at the crawling embarrassment, the hopelessness and estrangement, that follows an offence.
>
> (Jackson 1997, p.15)

[17] There are claims that his name was attached to publications which denounced others without his consent.

Others point to the emotional and formal aspects within the music that indicate Shostakovich's ongoing resistance to totalitarianism,

> to those glimmering, elusive double-meanings that everything possessed ... he would combine the lyric with the grotesque, and joy with irony, while the weak voice of hope was filtered through the deepest of despair.
>
> (Yakubov in Aranovsky 1998, n.p.)

Lighting Designer: Guy Hoare

Note: for ease of reading all quotations from Hoare are (Hoare 2004b) unless otherwise stated.

Early interests in theatre

Hoare attended Ampleforth School and was already interested in theatre. Initially he was involved in scenic painting and then a gap in the lighting team allowed him to learn the basics. He became a member of the National Youth Theatre and then studied Classics at Oxford University. Unexpectedly a range of lighting possibilities opened up. There were few lighting designers in Oxford at that point but several student and professional venues. Hoare explains; 'it was possible for between twenty to twenty-five shows to be available and one could really experiment and practise - assisting other designers and watching other stuff. It was a real process of discovery'.

The first contemporary dance piece

After graduating from Oxford University in 1997 he moved to London. Initially his work was for theatre but in 1999 he was commissioned by Longborough Festival Opera to design lights for Wagner's *Das Rheingold* and *Die Walkür*. He was introduced to the choreographer Mark Bruce and lit *Dive* for him; Hoare's first contemporary dance piece. He explains that he watched rehearsals of figures moving to a soundtrack and then talked to Bruce about it; 'surprisingly the images made sense to Mark too'. In fact he had wanted to light dance for a long time;

> although I had approached theatre first I feel that looking back my method then was almost more appropriate for dance. I was interested in where in space the actors were and where they were moving to rather than being tied to text or context. Dance was a logical step.
>
> (Hoare 2004b)

Henri Oguike

Hoare began to work with Henri Oguike in 2000, lighting *A moment of give*, *Prime Origin*, and *Ile Aye* for their first UK tour. Hoare explains that although all three pieces had been made previously Oguike gave him a blank canvas and allowed him to 'feel free to do my own thing'. During these early years with the company Hoare also attended the influential workshops being given by lighting designer, Michael Hulls, and choreographer, Russell Maliphant, which gave him ' a glimpse into working with a different process – a process that could start with lights'. Hulls (who had also studied with the seminal lighting designer, Jennifer Tipton in New York) and Maliphant were pioneering the use of light as a starting point for choreography. Hoare had been trained to light choreography after it had been made but now with Oguike he felt able to explore a broader approach.

Shot Flow (2001) and structure

Shot Flow was the first piece that Hoare made with Oguike after attending the workshops and where he was able to attend the rehearsal process. There were limitations in the amount of light that could be used because of the small theatres to which the company toured. He turned this need for economy to advantage and created a basic skeleton of six lights; 'this might seem a sparse amount but even one light has a variety of states. I exhaust the possibilities of each light in turn before I add another. A lesson learned from the workshops'. He decided not to change the lights at set points in the piece but at a place that could evolve and change. The music was played live and therefore 'if the lighting was live we could all feed off each other'. This was innovative and possible because Hoare is also the technical manager on tour and operates the lights himself. Critics were mostly positive in their response.

> In this three-way collaboration between sound, light and movement, the darkened stage is sculpted with beams and squares of greenish light. It sparks and glows as it catches the hands of the musician playing on a huge amplified xylophone, and glances off the two dancers.
>
> (Mackrell 2001, n.p.)

Hoare feels that the lighting in this work is a major structuring feature.; 'strip away the lighting and the performance doesn't make sense. The choreography is only taking place in whatever part of the body is in the light' (Hutera 2002, p.43). It also produces a powerful emotional effect. The beams of light glance off different body parts and 'each dancer is revealing and concealing the other person ... literally shadowing them' (Hutera 2002, p.43). A similar approach was used for *In broken tendrils* (2002) where 'some dancers move restlessly out of sight before low light, inducing a mood of fluctuation and ambiguity' (Hutera 2002, p.43).

F.P.S. Part 2 (2004) – flexibility and economy

Hoare continues to use no cue sheet in his work for Oguike; 'I know it so well that when to change the lights becomes an innate sense. Live lighting is a different relationship. I can be far more fluid with what I'm doing'. This also allows Oguike to develop the piece so it can continue to evolve during a tour as it begins to bed down. This adventurous approach extends design into areas that it cannot usually go. Hoare now thinks it would feel too restrictive just to light a piece and then set it permanently. He is able to be responsive to the live element of performance 'like the movement does'. *F.P.S Parts1 and 2* for example illustrates these two key approaches for Hoare; flexibility and economy. In this piece he responds to either the music or the movement and decides how it feels rather than following set lighting cues. Also he plays with a small set of ingredients; 'an economy of scale'. Four window-like panes of light were used for the opening solo when it was originally made in 2001 (see the illustrations on pages 1 and 24). Hoare plays with this idea again for the duet which forms the second part.

Other typical characteristics

Typically painting is a key influence, particularly Abstract Impressionism is of interest to him. Hoare notes painters such as Klein, Rothko and Mondrian who use large blocks of solid colour 'which forces an emotional response, similar to my response to music'. He is self taught in respect of music and reflects its moods rather than having an academic approach. Hoare explains; 'colour and texture is what is important to me. The choreography often suggests the shape of the lighting while the music indicates the colour and shifts in lighting intensity'. Not wanting this to be too predictable, he explains that this may also be vice versa.

Hoare is a regular collaborator with Henri Oguike Dance Company and has lit all their work since 2000. His other designs for dance include; H2O (HODC's sister company); National Youth Dance Wales; both *The Snag Project* and the recent *Snagged* and *Clored* at the Royal Opera House's Clore Studio where he is establishing another long term collaboration with Sarah Warsop and Joanne Fong; Alicia Herrero-Simon's *1/4* for the 2002 Resolution season at The Place; Charlotte Eatock; and *Just do nothing* for m.e. parker. He has also collaborated with the British digital artists Igloo (Ruth Gibson and Bruno Martelli) on multi media performances. He continues to light for both opera and theatre. For example, he is resident lighting designer for The London Classic Theatre Company for whom he has lit several pieces including *Look Back in Anger* and *The Killing of Sister George* and he works regularly for the Crucible Theatre, Sheffield. He also lights concerts, comedy shows, installations and exhibitions.

Henri Oguike performing the solo *F.P.S Part 1*

Designer: Elizabeth Baker

Early interest is in dance

Elizabeth Baker was born in York. Her initial interest was in dancing. From 1986-1988 she trained in 'classical ballet, jazz, tap, modern and national dance' at the Northern Ballet School in Leeds (Baker 2004a, n.p.). Following this she went to study at The Place, achieving a BA in Contemporary Dance from London Contemporary Dance School (LCDS) in 1992. Her interest in costume design stems from here. There were many opportunities to study aspects of production (costume, set, lighting) during the course.

The costume department at LCDS

From 1992-1993 she continued her study of contemporary dance at LCDS by taking an MA. This was a significant year in which she also worked with Jenny Henry who ran their costume department. Henry was not just a wardrobe mistress, she was also a designer, creating costumes for Richard Alston's *Doublework* (1978), Christopher Bannerman's *Sand Steps* (1979) and Siobhan Davies's *Then You Can only Sing* (1978). As part of the MA course, Baker designed Richard Alston's *Les Illuminations* for LCDS and 'made, dyed and painted costumes for CandoCo's *Flying in the face of ...*' (Baker 2004a, n.p.). She became fascinated.

> I enjoyed doing it and I was also choreographing as part of the course. How costume could influence the dance was significant for me. I had not intended to focus on costume design perhaps but I was also dancing in a small company and so came at it from a dancer's point of view. It can influence the whole way you hold the body. LCDS had the back catalogue to 1967 of all Robert Cohan's costumes for London Contemporary Dance Theatre. I was intrigued by it all.
>
> (Baker 2004b)

Designing for Richard Alston and others

In 1995 she joined The Place costume department, initially as a costume assistant for LCDS and then as wardrobe mistress for the Richard Alston Dance Company too. For him for example she created *Fever* (2001), *Tremor* (2000), *A Sudden Exit* (1999), *Slow Airs* (*Almost All*) (1999), *Red Run* (1998), *Rumours, Visions* (1996), and *Okho* (1996). She also had the opportunity to work with a variety of guest choreographers brought in to create pieces for LCDS including Lea Anderson and Martin Lawrence. She also designed independently for others such as Khamlane Halsakda and Magpie Dance Company.

Henri Oguike

At this time she also met Henri Oguike who was still a dancer with Richard Alston Dance Company. She made her first costumes for Oguike, *Spool of Threads*, in 1997. From 2002 she has been freelance, creating Richard Alston's redesign of *Dangerous Liaisons* for Scottish Ballet (2003), Tamara McLorg's *Unheard Song* (2003) and Roy Campbell-Moore's *Between* for Diversions Dance Company. She is a regular collaborator with Henri Oguike Dance Company having designed all their costumes to date.

Her typical design process

Her usual design process is to 'listen to the music ... before rehearsals begin. This allows me to gather together some initial ideas and gain a feel for the mood of the work' (Baker 2004a, n.p.). A personal approach is thus first sought. She then attends rehearsals in order to understand how Oguike is interpreting the music and to ascertain whether he is making a narrative or abstract treatment. Oguike also of course has ideas of how the work might look which she discusses with him and she also takes into consideration 'if there is any movement quality or body part that the costumes could be used to emphasise' (Baker 2004a, n.p.). Her own experience of dance training is useful too. She then makes samples (toiles) for the dancers to try out in rehearsals so she 'can see how the shape starts to inform their movement' (Baker 2004a, n.p.) Costume supports the other elements. Her desire is to find an individual look and colour specific to each work that is in sympathy with the dance, its vocabulary and its mood. In Oguike's *White Space* (2004) for example the 'mincing walks, courtly flourishes and extravagant gestures ... [are] lavishly choreographed doodles, allowing the baroque ornamentation of the music to take on absurd human form' (Mackrell 2004). In this dance Baker's white costumes 'cut sharp, but with a slightly unwholesome sheen, a subversive sweatiness' add to the air of cynicism, affectation and hypocrisy created by the movement (Jays 2004, p.37).

Part 2
Background Contexts

Contemporary dance

• *A brief history of the development of contemporary dance in England*

• *Some key resources*

The opening of *Front Line*

A brief history of the development of contemporary dance in England

The Modern movement was a multi-faceted approach in the Arts which responded to the new conditions of 20th century life. An emphasis on originality, innovation and individuality produced diverse forms. The early modern dance styles which developed in Britain had mostly disappeared from the professional theatres (for a variety of complex reasons) after the 1939-45 war. Ballet was the main form of serious dance and was very popular. Audiences for contemporary dance (as it became known here) were small, depending on visiting companies mostly from the USA. Thus in the mid 1960s it was American-influenced modern dance which took root. The 1960s in Britain were a time of social, political and cultural upheaval. Traditional values were being questioned and attitudes became less conservative generally. British society became more open to new ideas. When, for example, the Martha Graham Company visited in 1954 critics were mystified but by their return in 1963 audiences were approving.

American influenced modern dance in Britain

Modern dance thus established itself late in Britain. Two organisations were key. Ballet Rambert (now Rambert Dance Company) gave their first performance of modern dance in 1966 after Norman Morrice, the Associate Director, spent a year in the USA and then introduced Graham technique to the company. Christopher Bruce, a young dancer at Ballet Rambert, became the first home-grown choreographer to have a modern dance work performed in the professional repertoire when the company gave his *George Frideric* in 1969. Emotional content is usually paramount in Bruce's work. His blend of Graham-influenced torso and sense of weight with the free-flowing lyricism and gravity-defying aesthetic of ballet seemed radical in the early years when contemporary dance and ballet were considered, by many, to be contradictory and mutually exclusive.

In 1967 Robert Cohan, a former principal dancer and co-director with the Martha Graham Company, took over as artistic director of the newly established Contemporary Ballet Trust in London (Contemporary Dance Trust since 1970). Associated with this was a school, London School of Contemporary Dance (now London Contemporary Dance

School, LCDS) and a performing group, London Contemporary Dance Theatre (LCDT). It was Cohan who encouraged use of the term contemporary. His wish was to develop something distinctly British and not just to transplant an American dance form. He wanted to focus therefore on that characteristic of modernism that was more important,

> while this particular form, the Graham contemporary dance, came from America and is undoubtedly American, I feel it has to be contemporary and not attached to any nationalistic label. It has to be of the time and of the place.

> (Anonymous 1967, p.19)

Early alumni at LCDS and LCDT were Siobhan Davies and Richard Alston. His work *Nowhere Slowly* (1970) entered the repertoire of LCDT in 1971. Cohan's Graham-influenced idiom began to pursue a stronger lyricism and developed as 'a drama-based technique ... made more physically articulate than the original Graham' (De Marigny 1985, p.7). The style which developed at LCDT, although abstract, was infused with narrative allusions, explored psychological and emotional themes, evoked mood and atmosphere, favoured integrated design elements and used music as a structuring device or to enhance the mood. In addition to teaching choreography and helping to establish mainstream contemporary dance Cohan opened up LCDS to radical ideas and experimental work. He thus helped to initiate a fringe movement that also eventually fed into British New Dance;

> Within two years of its opening ... LSCD gave rise to its own counter movement. Graham-based work had been established as an alternative approach to ballet, but the counter-movement brought dance closer to recent developments in the other arts and to the new experimental dance in the United States.

> (Jordan 1989, p.3)

Merce Cunningham

Alston became engaged in this radicalism. His early work treated dance structure unusually and also included pedestrian actions and a softer use of weight than the Graham-influenced LCDS style. For example, the mixed media performance *Combines* (1972), an ambitious collaboration with film-maker and fellow student Sally Potter, challenged theatrical conventions. In 1972 (with Christopher Banner, Jacky Lansley and Wendy Levett) Alston formed Strider, the first independent company to emerge from LCDS. Alston's interest in Merce

Cunningham's technique, which at that point had seemed outside main stream styles in Britain, began to filter through.[18] He became increasingly interested in exploring abstract, movement-based themes but he also studied with Mary Fulkerson at Dartington College of Arts. This was a third important centre in the development of contemporary dance where contact and release techniques and other American post-modern dance influences were being introduced. This allowed a mixing of mainstream and alternative postmodern practices that was unusual at that point as choreographers tended to work in one area or the other.

Eventually in 1975 Alston went to the USA to study with Cunningham. Others also studied there, for example, Rosemary Butcher and Siobhan Davies. The Cunningham technique became increasingly influential in Britain after this as these choreographers found their own way of utilising it. Alston's style mixes: a Cunningham-influenced torso, which tilts, curves and twists; the relaxation of contact and release techniques; an on-going, gravity driven, fluid momentum; and the speedy precision and intricate footwork inspired by ballet. Music is key to it. Alston focuses on the dance/music relationship drawing on the musical structure and its emotional undercurrents. He was 'dismayed by the vague attitude to rhythm that he found ... around him in the 1970s [and] was impressed ... by the clarity of the link between melody and dance phrases in nineteenth-century ballet' (Jordan 1992, p.121). He does not mimic with simple music visualisation but also gives the dance phrases their own sense of rhythm and uses counterpoint. As Alston and Davies began to work in companies such as Rambert Dance Company (Alston was responsible for the renaming in 1997) Cunningham-influenced styles tended to become the norm in mainstream companies, particularly with the demise of LCDT. British New Dance and post-modern dance followed a separate thread of development and was seen as outside the mainstream.

Richard Alston Dance Company

The late 1980s and early 90s was a time of crisis. The economic recession was still biting. There appeared to be a tension in the mainstream repertoire between Graham-influenced and Cunningham-influenced styles. Audiences seemed to favour one or the other. Cohan retired as full-time artistic director from LCDT in 1983, a brief succession of American

---

[18] Merce Cunningham technique had also been taught at LCDS in the early years by guest teachers such as Viola Farber.

choreographers came and went and Cohan came temporarily out of retirement again. Eventually Alston, who had parted company with Rambert Dance Company in 1992, was made Artistic Director of the Contemporary Dance Trust in 1994. He founded Richard Alston Dance Company (RADC) to replace the by now defunct LCDT. Alston's work evolved subtly now that he was back at his roots. Unlike the Rambert dancers that Alston had been working with, dancers trained at LCDS still had the softer, heavy-weighted, more relaxed quality associated with Graham/Cohan influences. Alston's response to music now accrued deeper layers of narrative allusion and appeared less dispassionately abstract to critics. Oguike was of course a founding member of RADC and worked with Alston during this period when music became even more important (at Rambert the larger budget had allowed Alston to collaborate with artists and an emphasis on design had grown in his work there). In the video, *Essential Alston* (published by the Contemporary Dance Trust 1998) in which Oguike can be seen as a dancer, Alston explains how narrative and emotional content underlies the formal, abstract qualities of his work. There was renewed confidence again, in general, in contemporary dance. Christopher Bruce returned to Rambert as its Artistic Director. The recession was over and audiences began to increase. With the death of Sir Kenneth MacMillan in 1992 and a dearth of classical ballet choreographers it now seemed that the ballet world was in temporary crisis instead.

During the 1990s the contemporary dance landscape was reinvigorated from many sources, for example: British New Dance, which had developed its own alternative scene; home-grown and visiting South Asian dance artists; further waves of American postmodernism; and also European influences. The latter have become increasingly significant. Oguike notes his particular interest in two Belgian postmodern choreographers Anne Teresa de Keersmaeker and Wim Vanderkeybus. De Keersmaeker's best known work in Britain is probably *Rosas danst Rosas* (1983). She originally trained at Bejart's Mudra academy and then in New York where she worked briefly with the minimalist and postmodernist, Lucinda Childs. This type of style is characterised by its cool, rational and objective qualities but 'what set de Keersmaeker ... apart was her ability to imbue the repetitive minimalist structures of American postmodernism with emotional substance' (Reynolds and McCormick 2003, p.650). In the early 1980s her all-female company performed in everyday clothes and heavy black leather shoes which later seemed to set a fashion that others copied. Although she does not use identifiable dance steps, rhythmic gestural phrases are repeated using complex shifts in timing and dynamics to produce formal patterns across the group. De Keersmaeker has had continued influence partly because her PARTS school in Brussels runs a choreographic lab/project for professional choreographers. Vandekeybus's work uses overtly theatrical techniques, for example, his dancers also speak and use props. British critics describe his style as Eurocrash. They focus on his use of highly athletic vocabulary that includes diving rolls that crash into and across the floor and the real danger that is present in the speed and physical contact between dancers.

Some Key Resources

For further information about contemporary dance see the following:

Written Sources

For the full listing see the Bibliography:

(Ayers 2002); (Bannerman 1996); (Clarke and Crisp 1989); (Copeland 2004); (Kane 1989); (Kostelanetz 1992); (McDonagh 1990); (Jordan 1989); (Jordan 1992); (Mackrell 1992); (Polzer 2004); (Pritchard 1996); (Sanders 1993); (Sanders 1997); (Sanders 2002).

Visual Resources

Essential Alston. A Choreographer Discusses His Work. Lecture demonstration, interview, extracts from works. Contemporary Dance Trust, 1998. The Place, 17, Duke's Road, London, WC1H 9PY.

Alston in Overdrive. Lecture demonstration, interviews, performance of Overdrive. Contemporary Dance Trust, 2004. The Place, 17, Duke's Road, London, WC1H 9PY.

Pulcinella. Video from www.dancebooks.co.uk or www.dancing-times.co.uk.

Soda Lake. Video and resource pack from National Resource Centre for Dance, University of Surrey, Guildford. GU2 7XH, www.surrey.ac.uk/NRCD.

For Anne Teresa de Keersmaeker see;

Achterland; Hoppla!; Rosas danst Rosas; or *Fase*, videos available from www.dancebooks.co.uk or www.dancing-times.co.uk.

(There is no easily accessible visual material for Wim Vandekeybus.)

Part 3
Starting Points for *Front Line*

The contributions of the elements

- *Choreography*

- *Music*

- *Lighting design*

- *Costumes*

The transition to Section 2 of *Front Line*, Charlotte Eatock contrasts with the ensemble

The Choreography

Front Line was the second piece that Oguike made for the Companhia Portuguesa de Bailado Contemporaneo in Lisbon. Having not been completely satisfied with the outcome of the lighting for his first piece with them, *Seen of Angels* (2000), he decided to have a preparatory plan for the lights when he went to make *Front Line*. He developed the concept of marking out the lines/spaces of the musical stave. Having arrived in Lisbon he spoke with Hoare on the phone to get advice about technical issues; for example, 'what width of lines we could get, how to make them crisp and sharp, the actual types of lights to use so I could go in with the right technical specification'. He also wanted different shades of blue, deep to light tones, shading through from front to back and vice versa. It did not work quite as he had imagined it, so the palest blue/white was used instead. Oguike's lighting concept had an impact on his studio work and influenced the choreography from the outset. The idea of reproducing 'the graphic shape of a musical manuscript itself, in a direct translation, established the spatial values to influence the dance' and was particularly significant for the opening (Oguike 2004). Other movements in the piece were also envisaged as having specific lighting effects, for example, the highlight on the hand shivering/quivering when the dancers stand in a line upstage and then drop to the stage into the light in section 3.

Oguike wanted to use one of Shostakovich's string quartets. He looked for some rhythmical passages first to narrow down the choice (there are fifteen quartets) and decided on the 9th. He made his own analysis of the music, 'writing out the rhythmical patterns in simple notation to make it easier to see' and not referring to the musical score until he reworked it in the UK (Oguike 2004). He can thus visualise one rhythmical line against another and begin to translate this into dance lines. He began *Front Line* with eight dancers but an injury resulted in having to rework it for seven. For his own company this reduced to six, 'which seems the ideal number' (Oguike 2004). The central section was originally a quartet in Lisbon so Oguike reworked the material to produce duets and a trio instead for the UK version.

Oguike's first response was to the music. Having used Shostakovich's Second Piano Trio in *A moment of give* (1999) he felt that some of the motifs used in this previous work were appropriate to develop further. Three key motifs from *A moment of give* are present in the opening of *Front Line*. 1. A short phrase using three energetic side to side steps, which dig into place with exaggerated running arms, followed by a quick weight shift onto the right leg, torso leaning sideways over it and almost jazzy out-flung arms. 2. Small, terre à terre shunting steps, which push and pull the weight quickly backwards and forwards, feet and legs close together in parallel position. 3. A short phrase in which a smooth rond de jambe action draws around a gesturing leg, foot flexed in a low level circle which then steps out assertively into a wide, straight-legged stance. The weight is placed firmly out onto the heel, arms extended overhead, flexed wrists making an angular shape, followed by a hip pushing action.[19] These three motifs and several variations of them can be seen early in section 1 of *Front Line*. See in particular when five dancers re-enter from upstage stage right and walk across to stand in a block upstage left behind the male soloist (Nuno Silva, the dancer who is onstage at the opening).[20] After he walks around the rear to join them, a repetition of some of the motifs ricochets in deft canon through the group. In section 3 there is another brief quotation from *A moment of give*; Oguike describes this as originally being like a sprinter balanced in a ready-steady-go position but on their fists, its effect had been as a symbol of endurance. This seemed equally appropriate to *Front Line*. In section 2 Sarah Storer does this after her second duo with Nuno Silva. A similar action (although not on the knuckles) is used in both the solos in section 3. The dancers appear to be pressed down by a heavy weight against which they struggle to rise. It is particularly highlighted in Nuno Silva's final solo just before the lights fade. He clenches his fist and pushes himself up by his knuckles from his splayed position on the ground, to balance in one final press up.

Oguike does more than merely visualise the rhythmic tempo of the music. The shivering sound of the violin is echoed in the shaking/quivering hands of the dancers, which in turn mimics the actual movements of the musicians' hands as they play the notes. His *points work* process is used in the section 3 solos where material was generated by relating joints to points both inside and outside the space that the body inhabits, using direct and indirect pathways. The task was explored in a functional way, *points work* is usually improvised in silence so 'you can be more aware of the audible aspect of the movement' (Oguike 2004). He also finds it important to counter the emotional and narrative instincts initially in order to connect with an abstract response. The music provides a strict structural framework as well as an emotionally charged sound.

Initially the material for *Front Line* had been created on a classical company. In spite of the suggestion carried in their name the Companhia Portuguesa de Bailado Contemporaneo

---

[19] Ballet terms: terre à terre indicates small elevations where the feet stay close to the ground, having an earthy , grounded quality if performed on the spot, or skimming if travelled; rond de jambe involves a semi circle or full circular gesture of the leg.

[20] Stage directions are given from the dancer's point of view. See appendix 4.

were ballet trained and had only limited knowledge of contemporary dance. 'Spinning and spiralling was a habit with them, with full body involvement. They were soft on their feet so dropping into their weight and being flat footed was difficult for them. I had to really emphasise this and then the rhythmic ideas this created seemed to spread throughout the piece' (Oguike 2004). The manner in which the foot is placed down is key because it gives different qualities of sound and texture. He began to work with this immediately, exploring the effect of different digs, slaps, stamps, drags and pulls. He found the accents in the music and explored how the different qualities of steps could be used to affect the torso. How the weight shifted was significant too; 'how it pulled from side to side or gravity pulled it down and the subsequent response in the torso, like a puppet being manipulated'(Oguike 2004).

These considerations can be seen in the opening stepping pattern where there is resistance in the closing foot as it draws in and then releases into the marching step. The centre is also affected as the dancers shift outside their own comfortable personal space. The torso uses a Cunninghamesque articulation, different planes and angles are the result of allowing it to be affected by the weight shifts as the dancers concentrate on extending the travelling, 'the focus is strongly on getting from here to over there' (Oguike 2004). Oguike did not deliberately choose specific folk steps (although anything involving small stepping actions can sometimes evoke this) but he did allow himself to be influenced by the music in this respect. A lunge in a wide plié in second position with the weight on the ball of one foot was used for its angular, asymmetrical, frieze-like shape for example, although some have seen intimations of Flamenco in it.[21] Hands placed occasionally on swivelling hips perhaps more strongly allude to folk material but the effect is still subtle.

Oguike does not always follow the musical pulse and 'sometimes lets go of organised time' (Oguike 2004). For example, the slow trio in section 2 of *Front Line* has a looser connection to the music, allowing the thick, shifting chords to provide a heavy, sinuous dynamic quality as the dancers 'stretch, push and press each other around' (Oguike 2004). For the sharp duos he focussed on the intervals of silence between the pizzicato notes and explored the value of stasis; action and inaction are contrasted. The quality in the texture of the stillness matters, it is not simply that the movement has merely stopped. This produces a very tense, alert quality and also a series of ambiguous relationships. Sometimes the dancers seem to be challenging each other to catch or support body parts, at other times they appear to aim or fend off blows, sometimes they try to manipulate or control each

---

[21] Ballet terms: plié – bent knees; second position – a stance with the feet wide apart and at the side.

other, sometimes they need/seek contact which at other moments they reject. In live performance of the music this difference in the quality of the stillness/pizzicato can be seen to be different each night. Oguike plays with the musical pulse in other ways. In the third section of the dance he used phrases counted as 3 lots of 6, 3 lots of 3, 3 lots of 3 to drop the main accent into a more comfortable place for the dancers. For similar reasons, at another point, he used a slow count of 4 over the faster music. 'This meant that the dance does not always coincide easily with the musical pulse but the dance needs to have its own life over the music too' (Oguike 2004). Also the musicians sometimes take their cue from the dancers. At the very end of section 1 a female dancer walks around to the rear of the group before making a slow descent (the lights become red). The musicians are watching her and repeat their rocking motif ad lib until she is in place. This all indicates that simple, neo-classical music visualisation is not intended.

Even though Oguike had always wanted to use the title 'Front Line', the artistic director of the Companhia Portuguesa de Bailado Contemporaneo persuaded him to reconsider. He thought it might be too political and more significantly another Portuguese choreographer had made a work with an identical title. At its first première therefore Oguike called the piece *Of Death and Stillness*. The programme note that usually advertises *Front Line*, adopted as the title again as soon as it was reworked for Henri Oguike Dance Company indicates where the Portuguese title might have come from,

> During the final period of Shostakovich's life he retreated more into thoughts of death and stillness. The moods are constantly shifting, the instruments squeal like animals and engage in wild stamping dances. Elsewhere there is anger followed by listlessness.
>
> (Anonymous, 2002a)

Front Line has been a regular feature of the company's touring schedule since 2002 (see Appendix 2). Some critics now refer to it as Oguike's signature piece;

> His signature work, *Front Line*, is ... organised around fierce, linear tracks of movement. As the six ... dancers spread out in stamping single file, their percussive moves unequivocally beat out the music's violent rhythms. Yet what we register ... is the confined area in which the dancers move, the sense that their collective frenzy is beating against invisible walls. You don't have to know the history of Shostakovich's struggle with the Soviet authorities to feel the howl of claustrophobia embodied in the music.
>
> (Mackrell 2004)

The Music

String Quartet No. 9 in E-Flat Major, Op. 117 (1964)

'It had been four years since Shostakovich wrote his Eighth Quartet, whose haunted vision had been inspired by the devastation of Dresden in World War II' (Bromberger 2002, n.p.). The Ninth and Tenth String Quartets were premièred together in Moscow on November 20th 1964. They were performed by the Beethoven Quartet (founded in 1923 as the Moscow Conservatory Quartet). This was the group to whom 'Shostakovich had given exclusive rights for première performances of his String Quartets. They premièred all of the Quartets, except for the first and the last' (Way 2002, n.p.). The Quartets are generally seen to reflect the turmoil of his inner thoughts and feelings in a more intimate, personal manner than the symphonies for which he is perhaps more famous. During the last decade or so of his life, even though Stalin was dead, difficulties remained. The new regime persuaded Shostakovich to join the Communist Party,

> something that the composer had avoided doing all through the Stalinist era. Hoping against hope that reforms would occur (they didn't); frightened and worn down by bad health ... in 1960 he assented; much to the horror and disappointment of his friends.
>
> (Way 2002, n.p.)

The Ninth String Quartet perhaps reflects these troubled times. He seems to have begun a first version in the Autumn of 1961. In 1962 the Beethoven Quartet 'had been preparing to celebrate its upcoming 40th anniversary season' and expected to première it but the music did not appear (Weitz 2001, n.p.). Shostakovich later claimed to have burnt the manuscript having been dissatisfied with it. Unusually, since Shostakovich in general wrote with great facility, it was two years before he wrote the second version. This was then completed quickly between May 2nd and May 28th 1964. Dimitri Tsyganov, the leader of the Beethoven Quartet, 'recalled that Shostakovich told him that the quartet that he had consigned to the flames was based on 'themes from childhood'; the new Quartet was 'completely different' (Way 2002, n.p.). The new version was dedicated to Irina, his third wife, whom he married in 1962. Her father was a dissident who had been a victim of Stalin's purges.

The Ninth is relatively unique in its structure. Five connected movements are played without pauses: Moderato con moto; Adagio; Allegretto; Adagio; and Allegro.[22] The first four are quite short (under 4 minutes each) but the final movement is twice as long, contains new material and reiterates themes from all the others. There is a tonal connection with the emotionally wrought Eighth Quartet (a piece which some see as evidence that Shostakovich entertained suicidal thoughts at one point). The E flat of the Ninth is the relative major of C minor (the home key of the Eighth) and these two keys are held in a tense relationship. The major key struggles against the minor, only gaining supremacy in the final moments of the piece; 'the reason for the finale's length is the journey the music undertakes to achieve a tonal synthesis of material' (Matthew-Walker 2001, n.p.). Hope wins, but only just.

The first movement opens with the violin playing an oscillating rhythmic pattern, 'that sound – murmuring, rocking, throbbing – will recur at many different speeds and dynamics throughout' (Bromberger 2002, n.p.). Two more themes are quickly introduced: 'the cello's staccato second subject, sung beneath pizzicato accompaniment from the other voices; and the first violin's saucy rhythmic figure that completes the exposition' (Bromberger 2002, n.p.). This produces a restless and fragmented quality. The first theme, transformed, reappears at the beginning of the second movement, a slow and sombre Adagio.

> Seamless ... formless ... a stationary idea, too afraid of some undefined force to develop or drive forward, much like Shostakovich himself in his more terrified years.
>
> (Lozos 2004, n.p.)

The third movement, 'is a demented polka of sorts' (Weitz 2001, n.p.) with an agitated and unsettled sound in minor key. It leads into the opening figure of the fourth movement, another slow Adagio. This contains the oscillating, rocking motif from the opening of the first movement and also some violent pizzicatos. The fifth movement is highly rhythmic and strident in tone and uses counterpoint. It revisits ideas from all of the previous movements with bewildering energy as well as introducing a new 'folk-like theme in 2/4 against the underlying hectic 3/4 ... [plus] a breathtaking fugal restatement of the movement's opening material' (Matthew-Walker 2001, n.p.). The anguished sound of the violin is

---

[22] Only the Seventh and the Eight Quartet are similar, although the former has only three continuous movements.

gradually overtaken. The final ending in major key means that the piece is 'full of life and defiance' (Strachan 2002, n.p.) although 'for all the manic energy in this music, there seems to be little real joy in it. It seems to be dancing on a volcano'. (Finn 2003, n.p.).

Henri Oguike uses only the 3rd (Allegretto), 4th (Adagio) and 5th movements (Allegro) for *Front Line*. He cuts off the end of the 5th after the music climaxes and the violin drops into an ambiguous dialogue with the cello. *Front Line* is usually performed to live music. Quality of sound is striven for. At the Lisbon première a CD was used. At the UK première it was played by the ConTempo 4tet: Bogdan Sofei (1st violin); Ingrid Nicola (2nd violin); Andreea Banciu (viola); and Andrian Mantu (cello). They met while studying at the Music University in Bucharest and formed the ConTempo 4tet in 1995. Subsequently it has also been performed by the Paväo and the Carducci Quartets. The Paväo Quartet was formed in 1998 at the Royal Academy of Music. They have twice been awarded the Sir John Barbirolli Memorial Prize. The Carducci String Quartet, prize-winning graduates of the Royal College and Royal Academy of Music, was originally formed in 1993 and is recognised as one of Britain's top young string quartets. They were major prize winners at the Osaka International Chamber Music Competition in Japan and at the 'Charles Hennen' International Chamber Music Competition in Holland. In 1997 they were awarded the Gold Award at the Castagnetto-Carducci Festival in Italy and adopted the name 'Carducci'. On the video of *Front Line* the music is performed by the Artea Quartet which has also occasionally played for HODC tours.

The Lighting

Hoare lit *Front Line* after the première in Portugal. His telephone conversations, helping Oguike with the preparatory lighting design, had already given him some limited input and understanding. He watched a video of the première and kept the basic section changes and the idea of the pathways or lines of light; 'I kept the architecture' that had been used (Hoare 2004b). He also watched the choreography being remounted in the UK and listened to the music a great deal. In live performance *Front Line* uses a minimal set design and a black dance floor. The chairs and music stands for the four musicians are placed in a horizontal line upstage. There is usually a white cyclorama but not in the video; a bare brick wall is left visible. In larger theatres black drapes are used to mask the wing space. In the video, as in studio theatre venues, 'a bare, unmasked aesthetic ... complement[s] the raw, visceral nature of the piece' (Hoare 2004a).

There are three basic lighting elements. Firstly three overhead profile lights create the four linear pathways in section 1. 'Henri had envisaged the work in very linear terms, and four corridors were marked out in the rehearsal studio' (Hoare 2004a). Their width can be adapted slightly to suit different venues. The precise definition of these pathways has a hard edged crispness although each line overlaps slightly so that dancers are only out of the light briefly; 'this helps to punctuate the movement and helps establish a frieze-like quality to the image' (Hoare 2004a).

Watching rehearsals also established the places in the dance where the space needed to build; particularly in the opening section. 'The choreography staggers between different lines and lighting could be developed in respect of this. I used trial and error in the space and began to notice patterns emerging. I wanted to accumulate the lines as the dancers began to move upstage but not too obviously in sequence' (Hoare 2004b). For example, after the opening down stage line the dancers leap to the third line and 'the second line is warmed slightly as they pass over it' (Oguike 2004). Then the fourth line is lit immediately after the dancers have passed through it. At the start of section 3 the dancers surge forwards and backwards and the light responds in similar vein, with a 'staccato rhythm cutting from one line to another' (Hoare 2004a).

The effect on the video is of the dancers cueing the light but Hoare likes to keep things fresh in live performances so does not use set points; the exact 'rhythm and tempo of it changes, though the logic of the pattern stays the same' (Hoare 2004b). This way Hoare can respond to fluctuations in the live performance, as with his typical working method outlined previously. Thus the sense of rhythm and flow which the lights give alters with each performance. Hoare responds intuitively, paying attention to how all the elements change slightly and impact on each other.

A second lighting element consists of booms with three sidelights at the end of each linear pathway. These give the bodies of the dancers a three-dimensional solidity and help 'to highlight different depths of the stage and ... move energy around the space' (Hoare 2004a). When these lights are lower in intensity the overhead profiles glance off the dancers' heads, shoulders and arms, etching shards of deeply shadowed light across their moving limbs and faces. Colour is added too and gives 'the piece a bleak, brutal, sculptural feel' (Hoare 2004a). Hoare's emotional response to the music is key; 'it seemed metallic and also had a fragile delicate sound, bleak and melancholy. I wanted a pure and sparse colour like black and white. *A moment of give* had used a metallic silver/grey filter so I decided to use a similar quality in *Front Line*' (Hoare 2004b). In section 2 the sidelights also flood a red colour onto the stage and it is here that any comparison with *A moment of give* ceases. Red can sometimes be a difficult colour to use but it provides a dramatic shift for section 2 before the final section returns to the cold grey territory of the opening.

> I felt red was instinctively right. *Front Line* is a strong piece that could warrant the choice of a punchy colour. Colour sometimes has banal connotations. Here it was the Russian flag and again came from an emotional response to the music. I knew the general background to Shostakovich's music – the war and anger in it. Red also adds something sinister and provides a contrast with the other sections of the dance.
>
> (Hoare 2004b)

Three floodlights, downstage at floor level (downstage right, centre, and downstage left) comprise the third lighting element. They cast huge shadows; 'to exaggerate the frenetic atmosphere of the movement and the music' (Hoare 2004a). In section 3 these floodlights fade up in turn as the dancers enter the space so that each begins to cast several shadows. They crowd the space with people and give an air of claustrophobic oppression as they loom over the musicians below. 'Just when the picture looks like it cannot get any more frenetic, the quartet strikes a powerful chord, the dance stops, the shadows subside, and the space shrinks back to the first two lines' (Hoare 2004a). Shadows on a cyclorama were a key feature in *A moment of give* (1999) and reusing this idea enabled Hoare to make further visual references to this work.

The more usual method of providing light for musicians, putting the lights onto their music stands, was rejected. Instead four overhead lights, in the same cold grey colour as the dancers' lights, pool onto the music itself and have the effect of highlighting the musicians. They sit on the edge of its 'tight, soft-edged beam .. half-lit directly, and half-lit from the light bouncing off the music', (Hoare 2004a). Their hands are particularly noticeable in live performance. They are thus integrated into the total stage picture and rather than merely providing accompaniment they become a key feature of the visual design.

The ability to be flexible with the tempo at which the lights change is key to the overall concept in live performance,

> throughout the piece, the lighting, in conjunction with the choreography and the music, ebbs and flows; it expands to fill the space and shrinks back again to its starting point, the *Front Line*.
>
> (Hoare 2004a)

The Costumes

Elizabeth Baker, like Guy Hoare, came to *Front Line* after its first première; 'as the piece already existed ... with costume and lighting it posed a different challenge to me. The design process was compacted, there was none of the development stages spent in the studio' (Baker 2004a). Oguike had started studio rehearsals in the UK and she was able to watch the video of the première. The original costumes, by Liliana Mendonca, a member of the Portuguese company, were made after discussions with Oguike about his ideas for the piece. He wanted; 'something clean, something with body definition, to bring out what is there' (Oguike 2004). The costumes Mendonca created consisted of black jazz shoes, black trousers, a see-through tank top/vest for the men and skirts for the women. Oguike now thinks shoes were an odd choice and cannot remember why it was decided to use them. Perhaps it indicated the classical basis of the Portuguese company (the dancers might have felt more comfortable wearing shoes). More likely during the UK remount with bare foot contemporary dancers 'the accents within the footwork and the different uses of the foot against the floor became more important' (Oguike 2004). Shoes would have diminished the sensitivity of the feet to the different dynamics being elicited.

Baker was keen not to be affected by the original costumes and tried to avoid focussing on them when she watched the video. She wanted 'to find something else to do. Henri had the idea via Guy of a silvery grey look. Also he wanted to stick with black, which had worked well in the first version' (Baker 2004c). Thus she now decided on 'a strong sleek uniformity that mirrored the strength of their movement. I saw them as a small group fighting against a common foe. It was important to reinforce the severe and stark quality in the movement and music' (Baker 2004a). An all black, covered-up costume tends to lack definition so initiallly she experimented with an idea for colour taken from the lighting, using silvery inserts in the tops. She abandoned this because it detracted from the overall simplicity of the design. She left slits in the tops and instead gave the dancers silver leotards to wear underneath. This allows occasional flashes of silver to be picked out by the lights. Also a weighty polyester jersey fabric, textured with tight pleats, was chosen because she wanted 'nothing frivolous or pretty' (Baker 2004c). It does have a slight sheen, however, enhanced by the metallic, stark quality of the lighting. The sleeveless tops provide the required definition and allow the skin to glint in the lights.

Although Baker wanted to keep a certain uniformity she did not want androgeny. She draws distinctions between the men and women, 'to keep them as they are and to point up the relationships in the duos' (Baker 2004c). Although they both wear hip length, slim fitting tops to provide a smooth, continuous, unfussy outline, 'there is no flapping fabric to soften the stark look. The women's tops have a high slash neck line ... to broaden their shoulder line and strengthen their look. The men's have a high crew neck ... which by covering the neck gives a formality to the shape and in some way mimics a battle tunic' (Baker 2004a). The main difference is that the men wear neat fitting, straight-legged trousers to 'emphasise the length of their lines' while the women have culottes (Baker 2004a). These divided skirts look feminine. They have enough material to enhance turning actions and leg gestures but no exaggerated fullness to detract from 'the strength and simplicity' that she wanted as the main effect (Baker 2004a). Being knee length, as with the tops, the cullottes allow skin to provide a surface for the light to catch and glint upon.

There is no reference to *A moment of give* in the costume design. This work had originally used borrowed, rather pretty dresses. Baker had made more substantial dresses for it later. It did not seem appropriate therefore to make reference to it.

MEN

KHAM
NUNO CAMPOS
NUNO SILVA

FITTED TOP WITH
SIDE FRONT SLITS AT
HEM.
SILVER LEOTARDS WORN
UNDERNEATH

STRAIGHT LEGGED
TROUSERS WITH
ELASTICATED WAIST.

NEAT FITTING.
SLICK WITH NO
EXTRA GATHERS OF
SEAMING
"FRONT LINE" HENRI OGUIKE DANCE CO.   JANUARY 2002

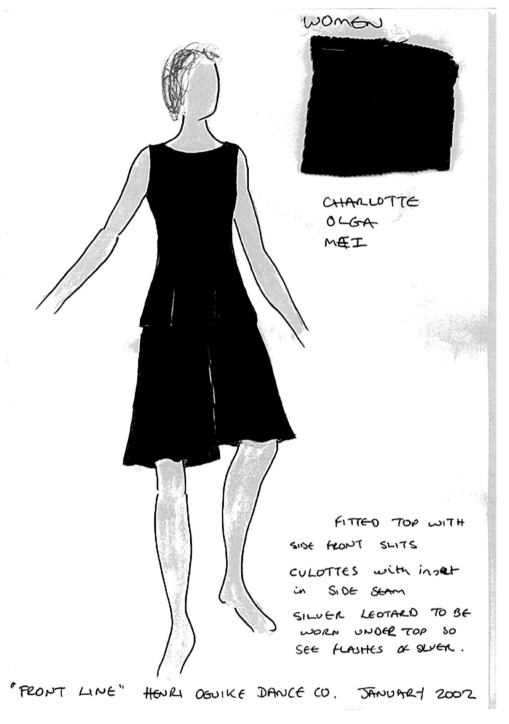

WOMEN

CHARLOTTE
OLGA
MEI

FITTED TOP WITH
SIDE FRONT SLITS
CULOTTES with inset
in SIDE SEAM
SILVER LEOTARD TO BE
WORN UNDER TOP SO
SEE FLASHES OF SILVER.

"FRONT LINE" HENRI OGUIKE DANCE CO. JANUARY 2002

Part 4
Using *Front Line* in teaching and learning

Ideas and tools for studying Front Line

• *Analysis Summary of* Front Line*: starting points, sources for vocabulary, style, key characteristics and movements*

• *Structural Overview Chart: a broad outline of* Front Line

• *Analysing* Front Line*: ideas for practical and theoretical tasks*

• *Making an Analysis: questions to guide the process*

The dancers cast huge shadows, the first major canon in Section 1 of *Front Line*

Analysis Summary of *Front Line*

Starting Points

- The music and its rhythm.
- Energy flow.
- A concept of four linear pathways derived from the layout of musical manuscript.
- Lighting design.

Sources for Vocabulary

- Quotations of movement from Oguike's *A moment of give.*
- Merce Cunningham technique.
- Contact and weight-taking techniques.
- Postmodern release/anatomical techniques.
- Audible aspect of movement.
- Folk dance (unspecified).
- *Points work* – improvisation process.

Style

- Contemporary dance.
- Abstract; formalist; allusive treatment of the theme, with some stronger emotional elements.
- Collaborative approach, all the elements producing an integrated effect.
- Similar material shared equally between male and female dancers.
- Complex use of ensemble; duo and trio work is a key feature; often sets a soloist against a larger group.
- Strong interest in percussive footwork and complex use of feet and parts of feet.
- A feature is made of minimal use of arm gestures in Section 1.

- Complex use of torso: Cunningham-influenced, off-kilter; allowed to be affected by leg or arm gestures; functional, decorative and expressive uses.
- Complex use of space: four specific linear pathways, stage right to stage left; upstage to downstage pathways also; diagonals, and some restricted use of space.
- Use of stillness; frieze forms.
- Spatial aspects linked to lighting design concept.
- Canon, unison, contrast, complementing, leading and following.
- Repetition, variation, recycling, recombining, motif development, entrances and exits.
- Strong use of contrasts - motion and stillness, open and closed shapes, fast and slow, near and far, staccato and fluid flow of energy.
- Non pulse-based/breath rhythm; music visualisation; counterpoint; audible aspect of movement.

Key Characteristics and Movements

- Variety of focus and changes in torso facing.
- Physical contact; structural/formal relationships between dancers; some narrative/emotional relationships.
- Spatial restriction and freedom; straight lines, proximity and distance.
- Direct/precise (leading and following; piercing the space); indirect/flexible use of space (serpentine, scything, dropping, shaking, weaving in and out).
- Strong, sharp, heavy, relaxed, bouncing, fluid, gentle, strobe-like/staccato qualities.
- Impetus/energy: flows or is sometimes arrested; tight and loose.≠–
- Torso: upright; occasionally with slight arch backwards; tilted; leaning; flexed forward; used to support partner; contracted, hips lead occasionally, usually a low centre of gravity.
- Leg gestures: deep knee bends; parallel and turn out; closed feet; high leg extensions to the side and in front; knee flexed; low level circular kicks; scissor kicks with elevation (hitch-kick); lunges; stepping into a wide stance (feet flat or on one heel).
- Feet: use of demi-point (rise onto balls of feet); foot often flat or brushes against the floor; raised foot is sometimes relaxed; foot slaps floor with percussive sound; occasional

flexed foot; ball of foot digs into the floor; heel scuffs out and supports weight.

- Travelling: walk; run; ball-change steps; spins/pivots; rolls and weight transference over different body parts across the floor; lunges; variety of elevation (includes – split leap with and without arm gestures; hops with variety of angular and straight leg gestures; leap sideways with gesturing leg flexing inwards; small jumps, backwards and forwards, with feet together; jump with both legs flexing upwards underneath the body); some off-balance.

- Arm gestures: variety of linear and curved shapes; closed and open designs; palms inverted; V-shaped arms; angular – both elbows flexed one arm bent upwards, the other downwards; one arm extended to the side while the other flexes in front of the torso allowing the elbow to point to the side in a typical Alston position; variety of Cunningham arm lines; arms overhead with flexed wrists, hands rotated so fingertips close together; pushing, pulling, contacting; hanging downwards; shaking/quivering/shivering hands; different surfaces/parts contact floor; initiate/propel/support partner; fist leads gesture and is used for support.

The transition to Section 3 of *Front Line*

Structural Overview Chart of *Front Line*

Teacher's Note: it is essential to identify the dancers. See the key below. The dance consists of three sections. The aim of the chart is to identify for teachers the salient points and a checklist of significant features in each section in order that they can guide their pupils successfully through the process of making their own analysis. The descriptions and interpretation are written in an accessible style but the teacher should determine at what point a pupil should see them. It is important for pupils to find their own words and be guided to make a personal response to the work rather than repeating the material here verbatim.

Key to dancers: listed in order of their first entry. Nuno Silva (NS) begins onstage; Charlotte Eatock, short dark hair (CE); Sarah Storer, white, straight hair (SS); Nuno Campos, very short hair (NC); Sarita Piotrowski, long hair (SP); Katharine Kerr, short wavy blond hair (KK).

Floor patterns and lighting	Dance Material	Structure/relationships	Music and interpretation

Section 1
Opening line:

1st Violin 2nd Violin Viola Cello
Line 4
Line 3
Line 2
Line 1 NS———————→

Audience

Begins in blackout. Lights fade up on musicians and then line 1. Clear horizontal lines in cold, steel coloured light, with areas of shadow indicated by dashed lines on diagram. Musicians stay lit throughout.

Opening pose: wide legged stance, focus to stage left, torso faces upstage.

Phrase 1: travelling pattern, stage right to stage left. Includes: Stepping and coupé action (ballet term: cutting the weight from one foot to the other) with delayed closing foot; torso drops over sideways; leap onto left foot away from stage left; walk forwards and dig foot, torso faces upstage; parallel pas de chat (ballet term: leap from one foot to the other, knees draw up successively); gallop forwards, arms extend sideways; step on the ball of one foot into plié in 2nd position (ballet term: a wide

Unison. A follow the leader line; NS begins onstage. Whole company join in, one after the other. NS and CE exit when they get to the end of the line. Punctuated with brief pauses and percussive accents. Little use made of arm design. Several direction changes along the main axis. Direction in which torso faces changes.

Dancer presents a narrow target; uncertainty and determination.

Lengthy phrase of movement follows the musical phrasing. Movement begins on count 2 so a syncopated feeling (accenting the normally unaccented beat in the bar, as in jazz). Movement adds its own percussive counterpoint.

Assertive and fast movement. Continuity of advance is interrupted by direction changes that slow down the progress across the stage. Determination to proceed. On parade. Like two dimensional paper cut outs. Dancers as a united group. Never ending line as people enter and exit. Black clad dancers like musical notes along the line.

legged stance with feet to the side, knees flexed); step back and close feet; two steps forward and dig; slight pause. Scuff flexed foot out, arms parallel in front; ball change actions turning, arms in Alston – influenced position (one arm extended sideways, the other flexed at the elbow); arms drop, ball of foot placed into lunge; close feet with dig; face upstage slapping foot down; quick turns stepping feet apart.

This Alston-influenced arm design is a characteristic position used by Alston – for example it appeared in his *Rainbow Bandit* (1974) and was used on the cyclorama in *Rainbow Ripples* (1980). See Clarke and Crisp, 1989, p. 121 for an illustration.

Changing lines:

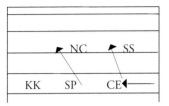

NC and SS leap into line 3; now two lines are lit. CE re-enters.

Phrase 2: repeat step coupé of phrase 1 with different facing. New material – brush sole of foot backwards, circle leg; step onto heel in wide stance; jump, jack-knifing the torso, arms swept behind; hips push, step over the support, arms in V-shape; small jump sideways, hips leading, arms softly flexed; small ball changes travelling backwards.

Phrase 2 similar structure and treatment and also repeats some material from phrase 1 but with new facing and directions. New material added is from A moment of give.

Phrase 3: NC and SS leap to new line in arabesque (ballet term: raised, straight back leg), parallel arms high in front. Two different and simultaneous phrases. Flexed joints and sideways move- ments; turns/pivots; walking and dig variations; a hop with gesturing leg in series of right angles, flexed knee and ankle. **Trio** – hop turn and pivot; heel on the floor; reuse the flexed gesture; high leg kick; hop in arabesque with over- arm bowling action. **Duo** – variations of steps from phrase 2 and 3, eg repeats end of phrase 2 - hands overhead, wrists flexed, jack- knife elevation etc. Also flexed knee lift, repeat of pivot in phrase 2. New jump with

Duo and trio in unison; complementing phrases. Variations of previous material combined with new.

Duo and trio pick out different musical lines. The sideways axis of movement is interrupted but linear pathways are refocused upstage and downstage. Sense of energy. Do not remain in one stage space for long. Some angular limbs give occasional appearance of puppet-like quality.

Duo and trio change places: upstage to downstage and then return to their original placement.

Two different and simultaneous phrases. Duo and trio in unison. Side by side relation- ship within each small group.

	flexed knees, heels picking up and slightly to the side. Perform different variations when they change places again.	Trio exit.	
Changing numbers: **Duo remain** (NC; SS).	Brief travelling phrase introduces new material, moves diagonally downstage: hands on hips, slap foot forward, step out to wide heel stance with overhead arms, coupé and flick lower leg back and up, hips push forwards and back.	Unison; side by side.	Folk-influenced appearance. Uses movement from *A moment of give*
Quartet change places – new duo enter (KK; SP) and change places with original duo, upstage to downstage as before.	KK/SP skip in; high elevated hop; leg raises and hitch kick. Travelling phrases overlap, eventually all face upstage - marching and hop step upstage; turn and move downstage. New material - sissonne (ballet term: jump from two feet onto one) with gesturing leg circling sideways and bending into supporting knee; small shunting jumps forwards and backwards.	Side by side relationship with partner, one duo placed upstage, one downstage. Own variations. Complement each other. Then quartet in brief unison. Briefly into a line again. Each duo makes a different exit stage left.	Duos retain their individual identity except for brief unison. Waves of entrances from stage right to exit stage left.
Soloist enters (CE).	CE arrives with repeat of last duo's entrance. Cunningham curved torso and arms; repeats shunting jumps but with dropped torso and flexed arms, then material from phrase 2 – running steps turning; wide stance with overhead arms. Exit stage left, as others.		The turning steps echo loud musical accents. Last one of a stream of dancers crossing the stage.
Trio enter from upstage left (NC, NS, SP)	Enter using unison skip with downward emphasis. Variations – step and leg flicking gesture from previous duo; torso tips sideways. NC – high leg kick; repeats material from phrase 1, plié in 2nd, travelling gallop with sideways arms. Stops and focuses on others.	Zigzag pathway. Unison which quickly divides into solo and duo. Two complementary phrases. Also duo in canon briefly.	Music building to crescendo. First crossing from upstage right. Flow of entrances and exits again. Skip retains folk influenced hints. Watchful quality of NC – not abstract, more personal.

A new front line (NS, KK, SS, CE)	**Repeat of opening stance,** NS in same stage position. Repeat end of phrase 2.	Brief unison.	Repeats opening briefly. Coherence, stability.
Solo (KK)	Group remains at stage left. Repeats in new combinations – step coupé, torso drop, flexed foot and circular leg action but then adds leg lifts with tilted torso, toe taps behind, little bounces with swivelling knees/hips, shuffles foot against the floor, hands on hips. Exit upstage left.	Soloist is matched with solo instrument. Variations plus accumulates new material.	Group watches the soloist. Dispassionate, uninvolved but percussive foot stamp as they exit stage left. Folk influences in the solo material. Irrepressible mood. Gypsy quality. Series of solos make their own individual statement.
New trios: NC, CE, and SP enter in unison; then NS, SS and KK.	Enter with step hop and dig phrase. Split into solo and duo as before. SP and then SS and NS repeat some of KK solo material. KK returns and repeats her solo material with addition of double hop on toe tap and adds end of SP phrase. All run off. NS left in brief solo which repeats material – hitch kick, shunting jumps, swivelling knees/hips steps, but new elevation with V-shaped arms, both legs bending in underneath in similar shape.	Repeat of solo with duo structure used before. New variations of material. Exits leave a soloist behind.	Successive waves of dancers now enter from stage left and cross the stage. Exits become faster.
First major canon: **Group** enters as a block from stage right. NS walks around behind them and joins at the rear to make a pyramid formation.	Repeat of phrase 2 material and shunting jumps. Also new phrase – stepping side to side with running arms; small step sideways, outflung arms, flexed foot stretches sideways then bends in quickly tapping, torso leans to the side.	Lines take alternating sides. Unison. Short repeated phrase brings successive lines into canon. Group shape interrupted by NS and NC running forwards, then back with KK. Breaks into two lines of three, exchanging places.	New material from A moment of give. Brief moment when all the group are onstage at the same time.
Large shadows are cast by the dancers onto the back wall. Then return to line 1 only.	Travel upstage and downstage then walk across to line 1 again. Repeat walk and slap foot.	Front line exit leaving NS in opening position.	Echo of opening front line.
Opening position repeated: Line 1 only lit.	NS repeats opening extract. CE enters and follows him. NS leaps immediately to third line to repeat the rest of	Repeats opening leading and following but dancers now cross and re-cross between lines 1 and 3.	Opening phrases but with new pathways.

Line 3 is relit just after NS arrives there.

the opening phrase. Followed by SS, NC, KK.

Transition to section 2:
CE solo contrasts with ensemble.

Line 2 re-lit.

CE slow balance in arabesque; runs forward, crouches and stands. Others join her briefly in line 1 step back to line 3 to repeat heel scuff phrase. Repeat opening phrase in new stage placements – continue to cross and re-cross.
CE drops out of group again as others repeat material from opening. CE finally in slow balance taken to low level.

Soloist contrasted against the group unison. Repetitions of opening material. Cross and re-crossing continues. Linear pathways as always. Brief echo of front line.

CE prefigures section 2. Picks out the slow cello and rocking theme. CE slowly resists but sinks to the floor as if energy is dissipated.

Lighting echoes the travelling patterns.

Transition links with ongoing musical sections.

Section 2:

light	
dark	CE
dark	
light Ensemble standing in line	

Lines 1 and 3 remain lit.
Red light added. CE in unlit line.

Ensemble walks upstage. SS stoops by CE and slowly raises her to standing.

Pedestrian quality to move-ment.

Gentle, as if comforting. Action tends to be more personal in this section. Control emerges as a theme: being controlled in a variety of ways and the need to control.

Slow Trio:
Mostly in the darker areas of stage left.

CE falls backwards and is caught by KK and NC. NC is always in contact with one or the other but they each break away and rejoin him as they travel and change level in space. Different surfaces and parts in contact as well as hands. Eg. CE separates KK by stepping over her joined arm and breaking her contact. They run to downstage left: NC supports CE in rise, gesturing leg in attitude (ballet term: leg is turned out at the hip, knee is flexed to make a right angled shape). KK walks to them and rejoins by placing hand on CE's shoulder. Focus is frequently down.

Smooth, fluid. Wavelike ebb and flow, undulating and drawing each other about the space, loose energy. Non pulse-based / breath rhythm. Trio with a single dancer briefly separated. CE makes a final and deliberate break in contact and walks away to stand facing NC. Long pause.

Echoes melody and tone of smooth flowing violin. Non pulse-based breath rhythm. Mood shifts: trusting, dependent, supporting, depressed, finally self reliant possibly even angry or frustrated. SS remains motionless – distraught at not helping CE or unable, perhaps unwilling, to join the trio.

First Staccato Duo:
NS strides on from upstage left to join SS who has been motionless at upstage right. Red light is turned off.

NS pushes SS joints to manipulate and propel. Eg. pushes on shoulder joint to initiate a turn; pushes shoulder to propel her forwards; lifts and drops knee.

Then SS initiates contact: suddenly leans into NS who avoids her, she falls. She launches at him and he catches her (see the image on the front of the video case). Then he leans into her, she presses against his shoulder now resisting him, her elbow flexes, they suddenly drop, he catches around her waist to prevent complete collapse. Hand contact makes percussive sound. Alston-influenced shape from section 1 is repeated. He grabs her hand to prevent her leaving.

Staccato, strobe-like effect. Movement is taken only as far as the contact produces movement. Tension/resistance produces absence of fluidity –bound flow quality. Tight energy. SS and NC alternate between ignoring and initiating. Restricted in space – on the spot. Tendency to 'close' in the shapes.

Contrasts with ongoing flow of the previous trio. Reflects pizzicato quality of music but not pedantic mimicking of rhythm. Ambivalent mood: avoiding, aggressive, trusting, controlling, desperate, challenges, exhausted, frustrated. Seeks and avoids contact. Lighting echoes sharp quality.

Slow Trio returns:
Red light is turned on again. White light at lower intensity.

Continuation of previous material. Stay connected, running, pulling, weaving around each other. CE remains on the floor, then KK falls from NC's grasp. He tries to support but then leaves her on the floor too.

Returns to smooth fluid quality. Zigzags around the space. The movement of one affects and responds to the movement of all.

As if the same trio was inter-rupted by the duo; replaying or repeating personal problems. Stuck in a rut; no way out. Reflects return to slow, weaving violin note. Interconnected - reliance. Non pulse-based breath rhythm.

Brief Solo:
NC at downstage right.

Lunge; gesture makes serpentine pathway, fist leading, torso leans; stoops and stands, fist taken overhead; fingers finally release.

Rest of dancers are motion-less.

Follows single weaving note in music. Hopeful and hopeless.

Second Staccato Duo:
SP enters and walks past NC.

NC abruptly grabs SP as she passes. Repeat of similar material to first staccato duo. Eg. He grabs her shoulder to turn her, they fall together shoulder to shoulder, she attempts to walk away, he grabs her hand. She now initiates: she clasps his

Structure similar to previous duo with SS and NS. Each avoid and seek contact. Different joints and surfaces involved. Bound flow and staccato quality. Focus sometimes confrontational sometimes ignores partner.

Repeating with different duo prevents the identification of specific dancers with a particular narrative theme. Generalises the problem to the whole commu-nity.

	shoulders with percussive sound. He supports an elevation sideways. Duo ends with sudden counter-pull which catapults them into an embrace. He walks away.		At the end they appear to hesitate, almost give in and accept the embrace but then NC abruptly turns away.
Changing numbers: Dancers regroup. Lights change – lines 2 and 3 are warmed slightly.	SS walks to SP, embraces her, the contact is rejected, she slips to the floor. CE joins KK and NC. NS travels downstage right.		SS echoes earlier interaction with CE. Unpredictable quality to human relationships. Alienation.
Solo: SS	Big, heavy lunging steps; press up position walking on hands and dragging feet; falls flat; rolling on floor; limbs slap down with percussive sound. Strides to NS.	Heavy, weighted quality contrasting with staccato actions.	As if in desperation, anger, anguish or frustration.
Continuation of first staccato duo: NS, SS	Repeats the shoulder embrace as with CE, repeats latter part of their previous duo but now she walks away without him preventing it. She pauses downstage left then strides back to him. Hand flings out to contact his shoulder; pulls him into lunge; they flex and lock elbows. They walk more slowly back to downstage left. He looks at her, keeps hold around her. Supports a long balance in flat arabesque line, holding the back of her neck, she falls away from his hold, collapsing to the floor.	Non pulse based breath rhythm. Uses the long weaving notes not the original pizzicato music. Staccato movement is juxtaposed to the music.	Again ambivalent – seeking and resisting contact. Aggressive, challenging, anguished, uncertain. Provides a narrative development of the earlier duo – she walks back to him as if to try again. Energy begins to dissipate as if emotionally exhausted by the exchange. She literally falls out of his hand. He is powerless to stop her or lets her go, uncaring. Sense of impotence and depression.

Duos express need for human contact and fear of betrayal. Sense of alienation and grief. |
| **Transition to section 3:** Lights darken in the centre. Dancers regroup on the very edge of line 3. Stand in a line. | SS uses fist supports to get up. Walks to the space left for her in the line. Stand shoulder to shoulder, arms open slightly in low V-shape, palms facing the front. Literally closing ranks with them. Slight pause. | Heavy, weighted quality. | Fist echoes *A moment of give*. Sense of stoicism and community. New line up. Section 2: more personal/intimate than section 1. Dancers focus on each other or deliberately look away. Slower. More restricted use of space. Some pedestrian qualities. Effect is more narrative. |

The group travel downstage in the opening of Section 3 of *Front Line*

Duos in Section 3 of *Front Line*

Section 3:

Red light off. Returns to lighting state of section 1. As group travels downstage all lines fade up then brighten fully.

Travelling phrase with linked arms. Jump, feet planted firmly into plié in 2nd; head circles clockwise, torso is bowed over; gallop sideways and run forwards; arch upper torso abruptly. Spin to split into two lines.

Heavy percussive quality. Sense of energy.

This section returns to the more abstract qualities of section 1. Group appears to hit an invisible wall as they advance downstage. Advance is abruptly halted. Sense of a determined community purpose quickly disappears.

Simultaneous duos:
NC/SS, SP/CE, NS/KK. Uses lines 1 and 3. Big shadows are visible on the background wall.

Two lines with own material – variations on phrase just performed. Eg. upstage line repeat plié in 2nd, fists brought to side of head; downstage line jump feet together and also repeat material, eg the slapping foot, from phrase 1, section 1. Back line supports front line as they hop past – diagonal leg and arm gestures. New front line repeats the slapped foot; new material – split leap to stage right; hop, arms outstretched diagonally and flexed across the front of the torso, leg in low kick. They travel behind the original front line who repeat the plié and head circle phrase in the opposite direction; two repeated pumping gestures rev up the phrase. Lines take hands across – skip in and away; counter-pull; supported jumps; direction changes; hold partner's elbow; plié with heels beating floor. Duos separate, exchanging upstage to downstage again. Phrase uses variations – deep plié on balls of both feet; diagonal arms from hop, split leap but with arabesque arms. Trio exit.

Lines of three exchange places upstage to downstage between lines 1 and 3 as in section 1. Alternating movement and stillness between lines.

Equality of treatment – female to female and male to female duos.

All movement except for supported elevation is close to the ground and with low centre of gravity to skim across floor. Unison and complementing between lines. Lively direction changes.

Martial pulse controls the dancers and impels them along. Boisterous energy but looks slightly confrontational at times. Returns to horizontal pathway emphasis again for travelling.

Briefly in unison.

A trio remains:

Foot slapping phrase – leg raised to side, foot relaxed and allowed to slap down in large action, hands hold

Sense of determination. Reflects the musical pulse.

wrists above head; shunting jumps; hop forwards with Alston-like arms, swooping turn with arms propelling action, attitude leg raised at the side.

Three lines of two:	Individual phrases of repeated jumps and hops, arm gestures cut in circles. Eventually SS and NC travel downstage – new variations used. Eg. circling elbows and pas de chat; high circular kick and spin; torso flexed forward with parallel arms reaching in Cunningham position. CE and SP re-enter with big high kicks and series of skips; repeat plié in 2nd.	Overlapping entrances and exits –busy stage. Creates complex counterpoint because of variations.	Dynamism and energy. Driven by musical pulse.
Simultaneous duos:	SP/KK and CE/NC stay joined, travel on short horizontal pathway, crouch over with front dancer guiding the stepping of their partner – holding ankle as leg unfolds; support partner as lean over back; repeat plié in 2nd and elbow support/hops material from earlier duos.	Simultaneous unisons. Supporting, creeping action temporarily slows the pace.	Many entrances/exits, changing partners. All short phrases reflecting fragmentary phrases of music. Echoes of earlier manipulation, controlling and staccato actions in duos.
Brief quintet: NS enters, duos continue.	NS enters with big hop; echoes gestures of duos. Duos repeat earlier contact material. Walk around and exit leaving KK, NS, CE.	Unison. Heavy weighted quality. Pyramid formation.	New musical phrase. Swirling quality echoes violins. High leg echoes high note in the music. Confident and empowered.
Fragmenting of group: Numbers change rapidly.	Trio in line. Sole of foot brushes back, circles out to wide heel stance from section 1. Also repeats flexed foot and sideways leaning movement from canon phrase, section 1. New variation - step onto balls of feet, hips push forward and back, torso ripples slightly, elbows flexed in front; shunting jumps; torso swings over and leg unfolds as body lifts; torso drops with arms	Unison. Side by side. Repeats structure as in section 1 – recycling motifs and combining with new material.	*A moment of give* material reiterated. Dancers refer to this as the 'Eastern European trio'.

flailing across and open; hit thigh and step into arabesque; walking on spot with hips shifting side to side. Briefly into canon: leaps exchange places. Repeat jump into plié in 2nd and head circle from opening of section, this time hands on hips.

High leg lifts and Cunningham influenced torso, leans and tilts.

Repeat of musical phrase but deep plié plants firmly on the high note.

Unison.

Sense of building to a climax.

:ries of solo entrances: uickly on and off, ımbers fragment.

Variations of similar material but one new elevation – a leap parallel to the floor. Different exits, eg. SS plants feet in plié in 2nd. SP and NC continue: hop backwards, parallel arms in front.

Duo in unison contrasts with soloists.

'S Solo:

ghts down. Line 1 lit.

NS repeats flexed knee elevation, interrupts the ongoing flow of entrances with slow, wing shaped arms. Repeats opening material. Suddenly breaks the recapitula-tion, runs to downstage right and falls prostrate.

Individual struggles to prevail.

E and SS enter behind NS. nes 3 and 2 respectively ht up again as they enter.

CE and SS run in one after the other from stage right to stage left – pattering feet, arms curved, frieze-like shape, fists.

Return to linear pathways. Arms reminiscent of sickle shapes, express determination. (Hammer and sickle – a symbol on the Russian flag)

S exits and re-enters.

NS uses fists to support himself up from floor. He exits. Duo repeat foot slapping phrase. SP and NC enter: echo of previous duo work. NS re-enters and repeats his solo phrase in brief, prostrates himself and exits as before. Duo continues behind him – support and contact; repeat variations of material – eg. flailing arms and dropped torso. They repeat NS solo

Soloist contrasts with duo as before. Heavy, tired quality of NS. Energy of other dancers.

Repetition of NS phrase emphasises break down of individual and community.

Echoes of the earlier control and manipulation in the duo work.

phrase but instead of falling to the floor a partner runs in to support an elbow as they tilt into arabesque. They gallop, travelling in a curve. Others exit, CE runs in a circle; NC/SS hold hands and exit.

Curving pathways are unusual.

Second major canon:

CE arrives downstage right. Introduces phrase: shunting jumps; tilting to side from canon in section 1; brush foot back and into wide heel stance; jump in plié in 2nd; foot slapping material. Dancers enter one by one. After many repeats, a final plié in 2nd.

Dancers repeat CE's phrase in canon, because of the repetition of foot slapping material several of them are in unison for these steps at any one time. Face different directions and randomly spread out across the stage. Linearity forgone at this point.

Random quality to the entrances. Feet batter out a cannonade of defiance and build a crescendo of sound. Reflects fugue form of mus - overlapping, repeating musical lines. Complex phrase in canon produces unison at various points. Phrase reprises movement from section 1 and 3.

The shivering line up:
Lines 1 and 2 lit. NS is in line 1. Others stand in the dark, only their hands in the light. They fall into the light when they drop to the floor.

NS falls to floor again. Dancers run upstage, reform the line, walk downstage. Stand motionless except for shaking hands held out in front; intermittently drop to floor and slowly stand. NS: roll and weight transference across the floor; limbs slap or drop against floor; raises up intermittently into press-up position on one hand, and stands.

Ensemble and soloist contrast. Ensemble: fast, small shaking; heavy drop which collapses in random order. NS: staccato and heavy; large percussive movement; uses stage space but restricted to lower levels.

Ensemble reflects: vibrato quality the violins, including the actual hand movement of the players; an the pizzicato cello notes when the drop to the floor – like puppets with their strings cut. NS reflects the quality of the cello and like th falls of the ensemble, his moveme does not always correspond in timing to the musical note. Non pulse-based breath rhythm. Staccato quality of NS re-echoes duos in section 2. Dancers appear exhausted as they try to stand but both groups continue the struggle Both groups are controlled by the sound, literally flattened and oppressed.

Lines 1 and 2 go off at the same time. Sudden darkness.

NS: still raising into press-up when lights go out. Use of fist to support. The ensemble are motionless. NC remains on the floor.

Soloist is reminiscent of Shostakovich's circumstances. Use fist from *A moment of give*. The dance does not end; movement appears ongoing in the final actio Determination not to give in, courage. The individual struggles alone. Focus on the music begins and ends the dance. Last two musical voices are recurring motif from across the work, eg. accomp nied the slow trio in section 2. La note dies away in ambivalent moc

Lights are on the two musicians as they each play the final notes. These fade as each musician finishes.

Analysing *Front Line*: ideas for practical and theoretical tasks

Teacher's Note: a Chart of Works and Themes at the end of this section is provided so that teachers have an annotated list of commercially available videos and DVDs that may be used to compare and contrast with *Front Line* and help to structure an appropriate course of study. The AQA GCSE Performing Arts: Dance specification requires the study of a range of professional work. The choice will depend upon the interests and needs of the group. Six major themes arising from *Front Line* have been identified to provide coherence to the course of study: music as the key starting point or stimulus; making a feature of duets and trios; percussive use of feet/audible aspect of movement; interest in set design and lighting; narrative elements; and unison as a feature. The AQA also identify a set topic for particular study in each year (see the Specification). The works listed provide a varied resource for this.

The Analysis Task outlines a basic analytical process that is suitable for GCSE. It is included here for non specialists who may be teaching GCSE. It is important that pupils are encouraged to *perceive* and *describe* what is there in the dance. It is an advantage to the learning process if pupils are encouraged to gather supporting evidence first rather than allowing them to rush into making statements about their opinion of the meaning. They should be able to *explain* why they hold the opinion that they do. Evidence needs to be gathered; a pupil's ability to give explanations and be articulate grows as a result of this. Interpretations are opinions about meanings and the effects of the elements that are supported by descriptive evidence from the dance. It is important that pupils are helped to observe and describe separately action content, dynamic qualities and the spatial aspects of movement and to recognise the difference between these different types of information. Structural and expressive relationships should also be identified. The GCSE specification lists the aspects to be covered in its subject content and attention should be paid to this.

The order in which practical and theoretical tasks are undertaken is left to the discretion of the teacher.

There are further resources listed that will need to be collected for some of the tasks. Read through the text first before beginning any of the tasks. The tasks are divided according to different aspects of *Front Line*. Practical tasks explore Oguike's work in a creative manner to develop choreographic experience and other aspects of the course as well as to elucidate *Front Line*.

Analysis Task: gathering the information

Teacher's Note: design an analysis chart to keep analysis notes in order. It should contain separate sections for different aspects of information. Pupils will also find it useful to draw efficient pin men/diagrams to encapsulate movement in some detail; make sure they indicate focus and facing. Make sure the chart is big enough. An example, which would need to be enlarged for use, is suggested below;

Section or other identity/dancers:	
Action content:	Dynamic content:
Use of space: X ⟶ Audience	Structure/choreographic devices/relationships
Lighting/set design:	Costume/music:
Interpretations:	

Method: watch the section or chosen phrase to get a general impression. Break it down into more manageable bits. Watch these several times more and make notes. The first step is to identify the movement content. The next step is to note the dynamic quality or kind of energy output that the dancer uses, eg. smooth, jerky. Speed and pace can be noted here.

The next step identifies spatial aspects and where the movement is performed, eg. size or level, body shape, direction, pathways, proximity. Then how the movements relate to each other in terms of their structure should be discerned, eg. repetition, motif development, recombination, with whom it is danced, complementary, contrasting, unison and overall structures such as narrative, episodic, theme and variation, ABA. (See the AQA GCSE specification for a full listing of subject content). Whole class discussion can take place as you watch. The teacher might guide this by prompting with appropriate questions, or pupils might work in groups to identify different aspects or components and share information afterwards. The teacher or pupils can reconstruct short phrases of the repertoire in practical sessions in order to illustrate and give experience of the points made in discussion. Draw stage placements and floor patterns as illustrated above. An X marks the place of a dancer (individual dancers can be identified by their initials); always indicate the main direction of travel with an arrow. Remember that when writing about these facts, it is usual to give stage directions from the dancer's point of view rather than from your point of view as you face the TV screen. See appendix 4 for clarification. Use the Structural Overview Chart to guide the analysis. Compare the two versions of *Front Line*: what impact does the editing process have?

Costume

- Describe the costume: for example, shape, texture, weight, size, colour, length, outline, fitting.

- How is the design different for men and women and what is the effect of this?

- How does the costume design enhance, or add to, the movement?

- Consider how the absence of footwear affects the movement.

- How does the costume design interact with set design or lighting design?

- Consider what issues are involved in designing costumes for this type of dance. Explain why Elizabeth Baker's designs are practical to dance in. For example: heat and expense, practicality of material, visibility to audience, ease of changing, general comfort in the fitting, safety aspects, use in the choreography?

- Is the costume abstract in effect or realistic? Does it indicate era, social class, historical setting or character for example? What is the effect of this?

- What impact does the costume design have on the overall effect and themes?

Set Design

- Describe the set design: notice details; for example, the bare walls, the placing of the musicians; colour, entrances/exits.

- How does the set design enhance, or add to, the movement?

- How does it impact upon costume and lighting design?

- Consider what issues are involved in deciding set design. Explain why the choice of minimal set is practical to dance in. Note the difference in choice between touring versions of *Front Line* and the video version of the set design.

- What impact does the set design have on the overall effect and themes?

Lighting

- Describe and collate changes in the lighting design.

- How does lighting enhance, or add to, the movement?

- How does lighting impact upon set design and costumes?

- Consider what issues are involved in deciding lighting. Explain why the design is practical to dance in.

- What part has lighting design played as a starting point for choreography?

Music

- Describe and collate changes in the music. Note for example: instruments used, tone, texture, timbre, dynamics, orchestration, rhythm, phrasing.

- What style is the music? What music and dance relationships are used? For example: correlation, music visualisation, enhancement of mood, sectional structuring, juxtaposition?

- Consider what issues are involved when choreographing to pre-existing music. What impact does this have?

- What part has music played as a starting point for choreography?

- Consider how the music and audible aspects of movement interact.

- What impact does music have on the overall effect and themes?

Title

- Consider how many interpretations of the title, *Front Line*, there might be?

- Consider the original title, *Of Death and Stillness*.

Practical Tasks

Task 1: explore simple travelling material

- *Oguike uses stepping and percussive footwork*

Take a simple 8-16 count walking phrase using a horizontal, linear pathway. Explore simple variations: walk facing different directions proceeding along the pathway; make some of the steps into turns; instead of all passing steps, close the feet, either with or without weight; make some of the steps into small elevations; alter the regular walking pulse to include quicker and slower beats; step out into lunge; highlight different parts of the foot; take some steps back along the pathway. Create travelling phrase 1.

Identify where percussive action could emphasise some of the steps or closes in travelling phrase 1. Explore how many different sound qualities can be made with the soles and different parts of the feet, eg, experiment with brushes in different directions, digs, slaps, dragging and sliding. Add any new material from this to extend travelling phrase 1.

Task 2: explore leading and following in unison
• *Oguike uses a follow the leader pattern*

Join with at least one other dancer. Choose one of the travelling phrases created in Task 1 above or link them to create one to perform. The leader begins; dancers join in one after the other and follow at regular intervals. Practice producing accurate unison. Explore a range of rehearsal strategies in order to perfect the unison.

Task 3: explore a variety of choreographic devices
• *Oguike uses recombining, recycling, and repeating to produce new phrases*

Use the Structural Overview Chart of *Front Line* to identify some repertoire examples to reconstruct. This could be as simple as asking pupils to observe a single component that they like, making them reproduce this or even merely approximate it, and then teach these to each other so that each pupil now has several components to draw on. They do not necessarily need to reproduce the order in which Oguike uses them to do this task. Make another phrase that travels in a horizontal linear pathway, travelling phrase 2, using repeats of parts of phrase 1 and combining these with the new components they have just learned.

Phrase 1 and 2 could now be performed one after the other if so wished.

• *Oguike also uses motif development and unusual rhythms*

Look for repertoire examples in *Front Line* where a simple movement idea is reused; for example, a flexed foot is used in different gestures, takes partial body weight and is used in elevation. Identify a movement component used in phrase 1 or 2 that can be developed in this way. Use the developments to create travelling phrase 3. Include in this phrase some recycling of components from phrase 1 or 2 not yet repeated.

Explore rhythmic developments: give experience of rhythmic games and exercises such as clapping increasingly complex rhythmic responses. Explore simple stepping patterns and rhythmic combinations.

Teacher's Note: drama or music teachers usually have a wealth of games to suggest.

Task 4: explore a variety of linear pathways
*   *Oguike also uses upstage to downstage and crosses between different horizontal pathways.*

Mark out two horizontal, narrow pathways. Use travelling phrase 3 and explore where a leap or other action could be used to travel the dancer between each of the pathways. In small groups as before phrase 1 and 2 can be performed using follow-the-leader formation. Identify 1 or 2 dancers (depending on the size of the initial group) to leap across to the new line for phrase 3. This also explores Oguike's opening structures for *Front Line*.

Task 5: create a short abstract dance with narrative allusions
*   *Oguike hints at narrative themes through using abstract vocabulary and linear pathways*

Teacher's Note: find a chessboard and chess pieces.

Explore the different pathways that the pieces use in the game of chess, eg. a bishop only travels diagonally. Create a short travelling phrase using the pathway and invest the movement with allusions to the character/role. Eg. use an arm gesture with palm facing outwards as if bestowing a blessing to allude to the role of the bishop. Make the gestures abstract rather than mimetic in a simplistic way. Ninette de Valois made a ballet using a similar theme, *Checkmate* (1937), in which the Black Queen overcomes the opposing king. Explore a variety of chess pieces. Create a brief plot or use that of *Checkmate* (eg. a description can be found in Craine, D., and Mackrell, J., *Oxford Dictionary of Dance*, Oxford University Press, 2000; Koegler, H., *The Concise Oxford Dictionary of Ballet*, Oxford University Press, 1977).

Teacher's Note: find an ordnance survey map with strong contour lines and indications of different territory/objects.

Use the map to identify pathways. Invest a travelling phrase with dynamic qualities drawn from the idea of travelling barefoot over the terrain indicated in the map. Gestures can be drawn by inscribing the pathways in the air or imagining the map is three dimensional around you rather than flat on the floor.

Task 6: explore a variety of partner relationships
*   Oguike uses physical contact and weight taking/supporting work*

In twos explore how pushing on a joint produces movement as the individual responds to the contact. Direction, level and force of the response can be indicated by the contact. The aim is to react to a partner's push in a logical manner. Two contrasting qualities can be explored – a sustained and fluid follow-through producing a lengthy slow action; or short, sharp movements as in *Front Line*. Experiment with different joints. Make a short duo using both of these qualities and question-and-answer structure (one dancer moves, then the other).

Teacher's Note: collect illustrations of dancers using different varieties of support work. *The Dancing Times* or other journals, books, posters and company leaflets are all good sources.

Identify repertoire examples in *Front Line* where one dancer supports another in an offbalance position, onbalance position and off the floor completely. Discuss and explore safety aspects of weight-taking material. In twos explore the repertoire examples and the illustrations to create a personal response. Develop a short duo.

Task 7: explore a variety of trio relationships
*   Oguike uses physical contact that is maintained or broken*

In threes explore weaving over, under, around and through each other slowly while maintaining a hand hold. Further experiment with transferring the contact to another body part or surface to extend the possibilities when hand holds become difficult to maintain. Involve changing levels and travelling around the space; one person can lead or pull the trio and the other two dancers respond. Experiment with deliberately breaking the contact of one dancer at the end of a movement. Develop a short trio.

Task 8: explore a variety of torso positions
- *Oguike allows the torso to be affected by leg gestures and uses a Cunningham-influenced alignment*

Teacher's Note: create a simple travelling phrase that involves a range of leg gestures but with an upright torso. Make a collection of illustrations of Cunningham or Cunningham-influenced work such as that produced by Richard Alston or Siobhan Davies.

Experiment with how the torso can respond to counterbalance leg gestures if they are increased in size, level, speed or force. Look at a Cunningham use of the space eg. curving, tilting, leaning, twisting. Develop the initial phrase to involve the torso. Oguike also uses an image of the dancers as puppets. Explore the idea of one dancer controlling the other as puppet master by pulling on imaginary strings or by calling out different joints where the string is being cut.

Task 9: explore folk influenced material
- *Oguike hints at unspecified folk styles*

Create a short travelling phrase involving simple steps eg. walk, skip, run, step and close, hops. It could be based around a simple hopscotch pattern. Discuss the five basic forms of elevation – one foot to the other, one foot to the same foot, two feet to one foot, two feet to two feet, one foot to two feet. Discuss safety aspects of take off and landings. Use different balletic or abstract arm designs for the phrase. Experiment with using different folk arm gestures from different styles eg. hands on hips, backs of hands on hips, arms folded and raised in front. Look at repertoire examples from a range of work to resource this. Eg, in Morris dances dancers might hold white handkerchieves and wave, rotate them or swing them. Combine folk and balletic arms designs. Link this with the phrase made for task 8.

Explore folk and other styles that use rhythmic and percussive footwork, for example: tap; Irish step; Kathak. Develop awareness of rhythmic use of feet and parts of the feet. These styles can then be mixed with contemporary dance approaches to produce new material.

Task 10: explore different group relationships
- *Oguike uses entrances and exits in different group numbers, canon with rows of dancers using alternate sides, and often sets a soloist against the group design.*

Use any of the travelling phrases created in the above tasks linked together. Two dancers begin the phrase side by side together. Experiment with using entrances and exit to vary the number of dancers on stage; accumulate dancers into a group unison; create a canon with dancers using alternate left and right side repeats; accumulate a small group dancing in unison and arrange a soloist with a different phrase which may either contrast or complement the group. A short dance could be created if dancers now step out of the group to join the soloist in a duo or trio created earlier.

Task 11: explore different methods to initiate movement
*   *Oguike uses framing, points work and anatomical concepts to improvise with*

Revisit the descriptions of *framing* and *points work* in Part 1: The Creators. Experiment with using these processes to initiate movement. Explore a range of exercises which roll and transfer weight across the floor. Examine the way that the spine can be used to roll, fold and flex in weight transference. Imagine being impelled by a flood or whirlwind that approaches from different directions and passes at speed to leave you prone. No sooner has it left you in one place than the force moves you to another. Recreate repertoire examples from *Front Line*.

Teacher's Note: when exploring any of the above tasks it would be useful to look at some chosen repertoire from the Chart of Works and Themes to elaborate on similar and contrasting treatments in order to enrich the pupils' responses. The choice is left to the teacher's discretion. The chart is annotated to assist the teacher in this. For example, when rehearsing unison, one could look at the famous entrance of The Shades in *La Bayadère* to see an example of the different aspects of movement that need to be considered: maintaining body shape, speed, step length and proximity, accuracy of pathway and rhythm, focal point and projection. Pupils could consider how the dancers achieve this and how they rehearse for accuracy.

IT Tasks:

Access the information at www.guyhoare.co.uk and www.londondance.com (click on Directories Menu, then Dance companies, then Henri Oguike Dance Company). Find information about other percussive dance styles such as English Morris and Irish dancing. Search the web for information on Richard Alston.

Chart of Works and Themes to compare and contrast with *Front Line*

(All videos/DVDs at the time of writing are available from www.dancebooks.co.uk, www.dancing-times.co.uk or www.surrey.ac.uk/NRCD)

Theme	Title of work	Comments
MUSIC AS THE KEY STARTING POINT OR STIMULUS	*Air for the G String* (1928), Doris Humphrey	Performed to the music of Bach. Modern dance.
	Pulcinella (1987), Richard Alston	Performed to the music of Stravinsky. Contains ensemble/duos, narrative episodes. Some narrative sections contrast with *Front Line*.
	Soldat (1988), Ashley Page	Performed to the music of Stravinsky. Contains ensemble/duos and narrative episodes. A Cunningham/balletic mix. Complex set. Some narrative sections contrast with *Front Line*.
	Still Life at the Penguin Café (1988), David Bintley	Uses the music of the Penguin Café Orchestra. Episodic/sectional structure. Abstract dance, music visualisation, with some narrative aspects. Includes a Morris dance. Ensemble/duos/trios. Ballet.
	Nutcracker Sweeties (1996), David Bintley	Performed to Duke Ellington's jazz version of Tchaikovsky's score of the Nutcracker. Music visualisation. Ensemble/duos/trios. Colourful set. Abstract work. Ballet.
	Sergeant Early's Dream (1984), Christopher Bruce	Uses Irish and American folk dance elements. Abstract work with narrative elements. Ensemble/duo/trio. Music visualisation.
	Intimate Pages (1984), Christopher Bruce	To music of Janacek. Uses his life as a narrative starting point. Duo. Music visualisation.

	Grosse Fugue (1971), Hans van Manen	To music of Beethoven. Abstract modern dance.
Note: see comments column for listings of non pulse based, narrative, chance-based and juxtaposition uses of music for contrast with *Front Line*.	*Les Sylphides* (1907), Michel Fokine	To the music of Chopin. A quintessential music visualisation, abstract ballet. Ensemble/duos.
	Sleeping Beauty (1890), Marius Petipa (also Swan Lake (1895) and La Bayadère (1877))	Act 3: the Wedding contains a number of divertissements. Music visualisation is key.
MAKES A FEATURE OF DUETS AND TRIOS	*Ghost Dances* (1981), Christopher Bruce	Duo and trio work. Narrative aspects. Non-pulse based and musical structures.
	Swansong (1987), Christopher Bruce	Contrast to *Front Line*. Strong narrative. Based on the novel, *A Man*, by Oriana Fallaci. Ballet with jazz/tap/social dance aspects. Duo/trio/solos. Non-pulse based and musical structures.
	Tales of Beatrix Potter (1971), Sir Frederick Ashton	Contrast to *Front Line*. Based on the stories by Beatrix Potter. Episodic structure. Strong design elements. Music visualisation.
	Strange Fish (1992), Lloyd Newsom	Contrast to *Front Line*. For example: trio involving two dancers preventing a third from sharing a wooden bench; trio where two female dancers in white wigs tease a male dancer; trio where a male dancer climbs on top of a duo and forces them apart. Some music /action juxtaposition.
	Enter Achilles (1995), Lloyd Newsom	Contrast to *Front Line*. See the opening section where a beer glass is used as a prop. Some music/action juxtaposition.
	The Millenarium, Wayne McGregor (1997)	Part of Spring Reloaded 4 series. Abstract. Explores highly energised, athletic work. Pulse-based and electronic music.
	Rush (2000), Akram Khan	Abstract work, narrative hints. Highly charged and speedy. Kathak time cycles and musical structures.
Note: See narrative uses of trio and duo for contrast with *Front Line*.	*Wyoming* (1988), Siobhan Davies	Abstract with narrative hints. Non-pulse based work and musical structures.

PERCUSSIVE USE OF FEET/ AUDIBLE ASPECT OF MOVEMENT	*Stomp Out Loud*	Dancers make their own accompaniment through use of a variety of props: brooms, dustbin lids etc.
	Stamping Ground (1983), Jiří Kylián	Modern dance. Range of solos/ ensemble/small groups.
	Les Noces (1923), Bronislava Nijinska	Percussive use of pointe work. Strong rhythmical focus. Narrative allusions, neo classical ballet.
	Soda Lake (1981), Richard Alston	Contrast to *Front Line*. In silence. Non pulse based movement.
	Troy Game (1974), Robert North	Use of humour. Graham influenced.
	La Fille mal gardée (1960), Sir Frederick Ashton	Contrast to *Front Line*. See Clog Dance and Morris dance.
	Memory and other props (1999), Shobana Jayasingh	Bharata Natyam: percussive footwork, highly rhythmical focus.
	Gumboots	South African, with traditional mine workers dance.
	Coming Home, Adzido	Uses authentic African dance.
	Riverdance	Traditional Irish dances.
INTEREST IN SET DESIGN AND LIGHTING	*White Man Sleeps* (1988), Siobhan Davies	Uses film of musicians playing as background. Very similar to *Front Line*. Interest in lighting.
	Beach Birds for Camera (1991), Merce Cunningham	Chance-based use of music. Uses brick-walled studio as one of its sets. Interest in lighting.
Note: any of the narrative ballets listed elsewhere also have complex, colourful sets that contrast with *Front Line*.	*Evidencia* (various choreographers for Sylvie Guillem)	Variety of sets and works. Made for camera. Interest in lighting.
	Coppélia (1993), Maguy Marin	Contrast to *Front Line*. Site specific work.
	Cross Channel (1992), Lea Anderson	Contrast to *Front Line*. Site specific work. Made for camera.

NARRATIVE ELEMENTS	*The Fall,* Darshan Singh Bhuller	Made for camera. Strong narrative based on the life of dancer, Celeste Dandeker.
	Nutcracker! (2002), Matthew Bourne	Reinterpretation of the classic ballet. Strong narrative. Use of humour. Colourful set.
	Peter and the Wolf (1995), Matthew Hart	Ballet, tells the children's story in clear terms.
	L'enfant et les sortilèges (1984), Jiří Kylián	A morality tale for children. Inanimate objects come to life. Abstract modern dance. Set/lighting interest.
Note: see above comments for works using a contrasting allusive narrative treatment.	*Hunter of Angels* (1967), Robert Cohan	Tells the bible story of Jacob and Esau. A duet using Graham technique.
	The Hard Nut (1991), Mark Morris	A reinterpretation of the classical Nutcracker.
	Winter Dreams (1991), Sir Kenneth MacMillan	Based on *The Three Sisters,* a play by Anton Chekov.
UNISON AS A FEATURE	See above	Examples will be found in most of the above works.

Appendix 1

Biographies of the Dancers
(source: H.O.D.C. with addition from author's personal archive)

Nuno Campos

Nuno was born in Lisbon, Portugal and started dancing at the age of 17. He trained at London Studio Centre (LSC) and was part of Intoto 2000. Nuno has worked with choreographers such as Darshan Singh Bhuller, Rafael Bonachela, Vivienne Newport and Michael Popper. In December 1999, Nuno was a dancer and choreographer for a Flamenco show in Sri Lanka and has danced in Resolutions at The Place Theatre for various choreographers and companies. He is also a Pilates and Flamenco teacher. He joined HODC in September 2000.

Nuno Silva

Nuno trained at London Studio Centre where he graduated with a Distinction in Contemporary Dance in July 2000. He was a member of Intoto 2000. Prior to his dance training in London, Nuno graduated with a BA in Drama at the National Conservatory for Drama in Lisbon. He has won, amongst others, the Centro Nacional de Cultura and Elizabeth West scholarship two years in a row. Nuno has worked with Kerry Nicholls Dance Company and had his debut as a jazz/soul singer in April 2003. In 2003 he choreographed *Tiana* for H2O to the Goldberg Variations by Bach. He joined HODC in September 2000.

Charlotte Eatock

Charlotte trained at the London Studio Centre (1997-2000), where she graduated with a BA Honours degree. She spent her final year at LSC as a member of Intoto Dance Company, working with Darshan Singh Bhuller, Rafael Bonachela and Michael Popper. Charlotte was a member of National Youth Dance Company (1998-1999) and has performed and created performance art works with graduating students from the Royal College of Art (1998-99), and collaborated with students from St Martin's College for Design for Dance (1997 & 99). Charlotte joined JazzXchange Dance Company in August 2000 for a project at the Royal Opera House, and in March 2001 joined Bimba Dance Theatre, specializing in South Asian and Caribbean Dance. She joined HODC in January 2002.

Khamlane Halsackda

Khamlane was born in Vientienne, Laos and came to England at the age of four. He trained at the Rambert School from 1995-98 after first studying drama and then completing a foundation course at Lewisham College. Kham was a member of National Youth Dance Company from 1996-98 where he worked with choreographers Wayne McGregor, Chantal Donaldson, Stephen Hughes, Bunty Matthias, Javier de Frutos and Jason Piper. His own choreography includes *Languages in Crying* for Resolution 1999 at The Place Theatre and *Corridors* for Evolution 2001. In 1998, he joined Richard Alston Dance Company and recently worked with Random Dance Company in their children's production. Kham joined HODC in January 2002.

Mei Lin-Chapman

Mei was born in Taiwan. She started her dance training, including Chinese Kung Fu dance, at the age of 5. Mei came to England in 1996 to study dance, drama and singing at the London Studion Centre and received both a BA (Hons) and a distinction for her Diploma in Theatre Studies. Mei has recently worked as a principal dancer in London's West End musical *The King and I*, and has also been working as a commercial dancer and model, performing various duets for BBC Variety Awards, Top of the Pops and Channel 5's Pepsi Chart. Mei's choreographic credits include Peter Williams Design for Dance and Pulse 8. She joined HODC in January 2002.

Olga Nikiditis

Olga is a South African-born Greek. Her initial focus was contemporary and African dance, but after a year at the Pretoria Technikon in South Africa, she changed courses and graduated with a National Diploma in Musical Theatre and Dance in 1988. After graduation, she was one of six dancers invited to participate in Options 1998 in Brisbane, Australia, and was nominated for the FNB Vita Most Promising Contemporary Dancer Award. Olga was a member of the African Footprint and Free Flight Dance Company in South Africa, and after arriving in London in March 2001, she joined Sakoba Dance Theatre for their Autumn tour as a dancer and workshop assistant. Olga joined HODC in January 2002.

Sarah Storer

Sarah began her training in Leicester under the direction of Sue Rosenbloom, before completing three years at The Northern School of Contemporary Dance in Leeds. After graduating she worked on various London based projects including a dance film for BBC2's season of dance and performed in several productions at the Royal Opera House. Sarah was a member of Diversions Dance Company for four years, working with many international choreographers, most notably Bill T Jones. She has also worked with Frederic Flamand, Director of Charleroi Danses in Germany. Prior to joining HODC in August 2002 she worked with Edinburgh based companies X-Factor and The Ensemble Group.

Sarita Piotrowski

Sarita was a member of Leeds Youth Dance Company for four years before training at the Northern School of Contemporary Dance. After graduating with a BA Honours in Performing Arts (Dance), Sarita gained an apprenticeship placement with Random Dance Company, and subsequently was awarded with a Post Graduate Diploma in Dance with distinction. She has worked with Wayne McGregor, Paul Douglas, Kwesi Johnson and Sharon Donaldson and has also appeared in commercial and TV projects. Sarita joined HODC in August 2002.

Katharine Kerr

Katharine graduated with a BA Hons in Dance Studies from the University of Surrey Roehampton during which time she spent a semester at Danshögskolan, Stockholm. She has been a member of National Youth Dance Company, 4D and since graduating has danced with Matthew Hawkins Dance Company, Double Vision, Dale Thompson Dance Theatre and Cathy Seago and Dancers. Katharine has been a regular collaborator with video-dance artist Deborah Tiso's b-movie group since 1998. She joined HODC in August 2002.

Appendix 2

Henri Oguike Dance Company Touring Schedule
(source: H.O.D.C. and author's personal archive)

date	venue	notes
2002		
* performance includes live music		
21 Jan*	Oxford Playhouse.	Not *Front Line*
31 Jan*	Crescent Theatre, Birmingham	Première of *Front Line*
1 Feb*	The Point, Eastleigh	
22 Feb*	Studio Theatre, London	
26-27 Feb*	Robin Howard Theatre, London.	
2 March*	The Arts Theatre, Bath	
5 March	Theatre by the Lake, Keswick	
7 March*	Darlington Arts, Darlington	
9 March	Southport Arts Centre, Merseyside	
13-14 March*	Mac, Birmingham	
22 March*	Town Hall, Swindon	
11 April*	Phoenix Arts, Leicester	
15-17 April*	Robin Howard Theatre, London	
2003		
29 Jan*	South Hill Park, Bracknell	
4 Feb	Studio Theatre, London	
6 Feb*	Wyvern Theatre, Swindon	
10 Feb	Studio Theatre, Chichester	
20-21 Feb*	Mac, Birmingham	
1 March*	Arts Theatre, Bath	
5 March*	Southport Arts Centre, Merseyside	
6 March*	Wycombe Swan, High Wycombe	
13 March	Theatre by the Lake, Keswick	
18 March*	Rhoda McGaw Theatre, Woking	
19-20 March*	Bonnie Bird Theatre Laban, London	
29 March*	Ludwig Forum for International Arts, Aachan, Germany	
12 April*	Richmond heater, London	
7-8 May*	Altenburg-Gera Theater, Germany	
27 Sept*	The Riley Theatre, Leeds	
7 Oct	Studio Theatre, Portsmouth	
9 Oct	The Barn, Dartington Hall, Totnes	
11 Oct*	Oxford Playhouse, Oxford	
15 Oct*	The Roses Theatre, Tewkesbury	
22 Oct*	Corn Exchange, Newbury	
23 Oct*	Taliesin Arts Centre, Swansea	

25 Oct*	Bonnie Bird Theatre Laban, London	
6 & 7 Nov*	Cambridge Arts Theatre, Cambridge	
12 Nov*	Gala Theatre, Durham	
15 Nov*	The Electric Theatre, Guildford	
18 Nov*	The Hawth Theatre, Crawley	
20 Nov	Lakeside Arts Centre, Nottingham	Not *Front Line*
27 Nov*	DanceXchange, Patrick Centre, Birmingham	

2004

28 January*	Wyvern Theatre, Swindon	
31 January	British Dance Edition 2004 Corn Exchange, Cambridge	*White Space* only
4 February*	Theatre Royal, Bury St Edmunds	
6 February*	Sherman Theatr, Cardiff	
25 February*	Kenneth Moore Theatre, Ilford	
27 February*	South Hill Park Arts Centre, Bracknell	
28 February*	Arts Theatre Bath, Bath	
2 March*	Gardner Arts Centre, Brighton	
4 March*	Nuffield Theatre, Lancaster	
6 March*	Bowen West Theatre, Bedford	
8 March	Studio Theatre, London	
11 March*	Contact Theatre, Manchester	
12 & 13 March*	Everyman Theatre, Liverpool	
18 &19 March*	Mac, Birmingham	
20 March*	Traverse Theatre, Edinburgh	
27 March*	Wycombe Swan, High Wycombe	
31 March*	Phoenix Arts, Leicester	
1 April	Trinity Theatre, Tunbridge Wells	
21 & 22 April*	Queen Elizabeth Hall, London	
1 August	Theatr Bycheiniog, Brecon	National Youth Dance Wales, *Spatial Signatures*
I Oct*	The Point, Eastleigh	
6 Oct*	The Show Room, University College, Chichester	
8-9 Oct*	Bonnie Bird Theatre Laban, London	
3 Nov*	Roses Theatre, Tewkesbury	
5-6 Nov*	Cambridge Arts Theatre	
9 Nov*	Lakeside Arts Centre, University of Nottingham	
11 Nov*	Arts Depot, Barnet, London	
12-13 Nov*	Patrick Centre, Birmingham	
23 Nov*	Theatre by the Lake, Keswick	
25 Nov*	Gulbenkian Theatre, Canterbury	

Repertoire of HODC tours above:
Tour 2002 *Front Line* (2002), *In broken tendrils* (2002), *Ile aye* (2000), *Melancholy Thoughts* (2001), *Shot Flow* (2001)
Tour 2003 *Front Line* (2002), *Dido & Aeneas* (2003), *F.P.S. (part 1)* (2002), *Finale* (2003).
Tour 2004 *Front Line* (2002), *White Space* (2001), *F.P.S. (parts 1 and 2)* (2004), *Finale* (2003), and *Dido & Aeneas* (2003), though this latter work is not in the Autumn Tour.

Appendix 3

Summary of artistic influences on Henri Oguike: see Part One: The Creators and Part Two: Background Contexts for further details

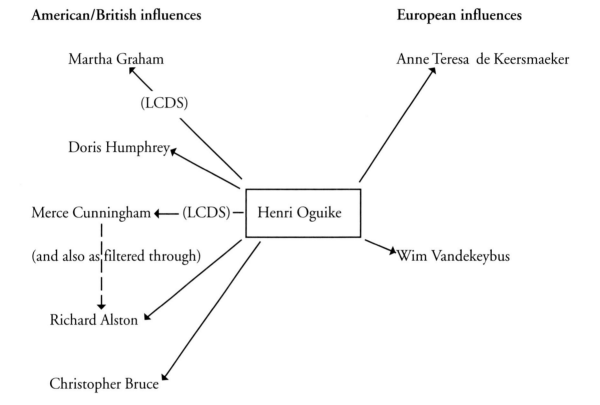

Appendix 4:

Stage directions/terminology

AUDIENCE

downstage left	downstage centre	downstage right
stage left	centre	stage right
upstage left	upstage centre	upstage right

Teachers' Note: stage directions/terminology is given from the dancer's point of view and not from that of the spectator.

Appendix 5: Extracts from reviews

'The dancers slap the ground with splayed feet and imprint the air with blunt movement. The effect is spectacular, but eventually goes nowhere. The choreographic structure lacks independent strength, driven too obviously in one direction and another by the music's dynamic'.
Nadine Meisner, Dance to the light fantastic, *The Independent*, April 24th, 2002, accessed 27/22/02, www.independent.co.uk.

'*Front Line* is a most fearsome dance ... the dancers wear classy costumes ... and fearsome expessions, clenching fists, slapping each other's bodies, making sudden jumps with slashing feet, keeping a stamping rhythm going with their bare feet like a drum-roll announcing the end of time ... I was lost in admiration when he turned a four-part fugue in the music into a six-part fugue in the dance'.
Ismene Brown, Music and movement magically married, *The Daily Telegraph*, February 26th, 2002, accessed 27/11/02, www.porta.telegraph.co.uk.

'A fierce and feisty composition ... dancers dart in and around the complex rhythms, caught up in a swirl of fervour and pugnacity, their feet stamping in a kind of ritualistic anger ... the choreography breaks down into an uncertain, quiescent surrender. The dance follows the music into a vigourous allegro, falling and slapping into a stirring finale'.
Debra Craine, First Night Reviews: Henri Oguike, Times Online, April 19th, 2002.

'Oguike's responses ... are always to his music, forging an almost mystical union between dancers and players. Apart from special funding for live music, he has few resources. Yet he and his lighting designer ... conjure gleaming worlds for each piece: the latest, well-named *Front Line*, treads the very edge if life and death'.
Jann Parry, Look out, it's another of those gypsy temptresses ..., *The Observer*, April 21st, 2002, accessed 27/11/02, www.observer.co.uk.

'bare feet slap the stage as six dancers and their shadows criss-cross restlessly ... plucked strings provoke a confrontational duet; a soloist is stranded in grief; the group is possessed by the music ... shaking, the dancers drop to the floor at the end, as though, suspended by the strings, they've suddenly been let go'.
Jann Parry, Hooray for Henri, *The Observer*, Reviews Section, February 2nd, 2003, p.10.

'As the six black-clad dancers spread out in stamping single file, their percussive moves beat out the music's violent rhtyhms. Yet what we register most sharply is the confined area in which the dancers move, the sense that their collective frenzy is beating against invisible walls.'
Judith Mackrell, Henri Oguike Dance Company, *The Guardian*, April 26th, 2004, accessed 05/08/04, at http://212.187.153.20.

'Oguike's jazzy brute of a piece packs a punch. This is dance with a spring in its step and a sting in the tail. Like a well-oiled machine, the six dancers stamp the floor or allow limbs to lick the air with a primitive, assaultive grace.'
Donald Hutera, Henri Oguike, *The Times*, January 31st, 2004, accessed 05/08/04, www.guyhoare.co.uk

'hops-steps with brooding urgency ... he resists the merely illustrative ... a title implying courage and risk, as well as the existence of enemy or objective. This tightly wound piece begins with flurries of stomping embellished, say, by a swaying hip. The music slows and the stage is bathed in red. A trio grapples it way through ... a woman disconcertingly flops and writhes about the space. The others are still, backs turned to her flailings. Then all stand in a row, arms lowered and poised as if in collective humility ... Oguike's bold dance has a bruised brutality'.
Donald Hutera, British Dance Edition, *Dance Now*, 11, 1, Spring 2002, p.74-75.

Bibliography

Anonymous. Robert Cohan; talks on contemporary dance in Britain. *Dance and Dancers*, 18, 9, 1967. pp.19-21

Anonymous. Essential Alston (video), Contemporary Dance Trust. 1998

Anonymous. Henri Oguike Dance Company Advertising Leaflet, Spring Tour. 2002a.

Anonymous. Henri Oguike Dance Company Listing on londondance.com. no page numbers, www.londondance.com, accessed 27/11/02. 2002b

Aranovsky, M. Sound-Allegories: a summary of Manashir Yakubov's programme notes for the 1998 Shostakovich season at the Barbican, London., www.siuve.edu/.../shosqt.html, accessed 05/08/04. 1998

Ayers, R. Scratching the Inner Fields: listening to Wim Vandekeybus. *Dance Theatre Journal*, 18, 2, 2002. pp.6-9

Baker, E. notes provided to the author, no page numbers. 2004a.

Baker, E. personal communication with the author, 20th July. 2004b

Baker, E. personal communication with the author. 2004c.

Bannerman, H. Choreographer Fact Card: Martha Graham, National Resource Centre for Dance. 1996

Bromberger, E. San Francisco Performances: program notes, www.performance.../.../asq2002.asq, accessed 05/08/04. 2002

Brown, I. Music and movement magically married. *Daily Telegraph*, 26 February, 2002a. no page number available, accessed at www.portal.telegraph.co.uk, 27/11/02

Brown, I. Whole-body dives to zen-like stillness. *Daily Telegraph*, 17 April, no page number available, accessed at www.portal.telegraph.co.uk, 27/11/02. 17 April, 2002b

Clarke, M. and C. Crisp. *London Contemporary Dance Theatre: the first 21 Years*, London: Dance Books. 1989

Copeland, R. *Merce Cunningham: the modernising of modern dance*, Routledge. 2004

Craine, D. Henri Oguike. *The Times*, 19 April, 2002a. p.21

Craine, D. Henri Oguike Dance Company, Robin Howard Theatre, The Place, London. *The Independent*, 24 April, accessed at www.independent.co.uk, 27/11/02, 2002b.

De Marigny, C. Siobhan Davies. *Dance Theatre Journal*, 3, 4, 1985. pp.6-7

Finn, R. Programme Notes, www.clevelandch.../.../notes_may4.html, accessed 05/08/04. 2003

Foley, K. How to start a Dance Company. *Ballett International*, 8-9, August, 1999. p.52-53

Frater, S. Henri Oguike Dance Company. *Evening Standard*, 16 April, 2002.

Grout, D. and C. Palisca. *A History of Western Music*. New York and London, W.W.

Norton and Company. 1996

Hoare, G. notes provided to the author, no page numbers. 2004a.

Hoare, G. personal communication with the author. 2004b.

Humphrey, D. *The Art of Making Dances*. London, Dance Books Ltd. 1959

Hutera, D. Bringers of Light. *Dance Theatre Journal*, 18, 1, 2002. pp.40-43

Jackson, S. *Dmitri Shostakovich: An essential guide to his life and works*. London, Pavilion. 1997

Jays, D. Resolution. *Dancing Times*, April, 1996. p.669

Jays, D. British Dance Edition. *Dancing Times*, April, 2004. pp.35-37

Jordan, S. British Modern Dance: Early Radicalism. *Dance Research*, VII, 2, 1989. pp. 3-15

Jordan, S. *Striding Out*. London, Dance Books. 1992

Kane, A. Richard Alston: Twenty-One years of Choreography. *Dance Research*, VII, 2, 1989. pp. 16-54

Kostelanetz, R. *Merce Cunningham: Dancing in Time and Space*, London: Dance Books. 1992

Lozos, J. Shostakovich Ninth Quartet, www.andrew.cmu.edu/user/jlozos/shostakovich/opus117.html, accessed 05/08/04. 2004

MacDonald, I. Music under Soviet rule: The War Symphonies, www.siue.edu/~aho/musov/warsym.html, accessed 20/07/04, pp1-8. 1999

Mackrell, J. *Out of Line: the Story of British New Dance*, London: Dance Books. 1992

Mackrell, J. Henri Oguike Company. *The Guardian*, December 13, www.guardian.co.uk, accessed 27/11/02, no page number available. 2001

Mackrell, J. Henri Oguike Dance Company, *The Guardian*, 26th April, no page number available, www.guardian.co.uk, accessed 05/08/04. 2004

Matthew-Walker, R. Sleeve Notes – Shostakovich String Quartets, www.hyperion-records.com, accessed 05/08/04. 2001

McDonagh, D. *The Rise and Fall and Rise of Modern Dance: the Story of Modern Dance in the 1960s*, London: Dance Books. 1990

Meisner, N. Henri Oguike Dance Company: Dance to the light fantastic. *Independent*, 24 April., accessed at www.independent.co.uk, 27/11/02, 2002.

Oguike, H. personal communication with the author, 5th January. 2003.

Oguike, H. personal communication with the author, June 21 and August 11. 2004.

Ottaway, H. *Shostakovich Symphonies*, BBC Publications. 1978

Percival, J. Henri Oguike, Stratford Circus, London. *Independent*, 13 December, no page number available, www.guardian.co.uk , accessed 27/11/02, 2001.

Polzer, L. Dance about Dance: Richard Alston Interviewed. *Dancing Times*, April, 2004.

pp.16-23

Pritchard, J. *Rambert: A Celebration*, London: Rambert Dance Company. 1996

Reynolds, N. and M. McCormick. *No Fixed Points: Dance in the Twentieth Century*. New Haven and London, Yale University Press. 2003

Sanders, L. Siobhan Davies: the development of a choreographic style, Resource Pack, National Resource Centre for Dance. 1993

Sanders, L. Choreographer Fact Card: Christopher Bruce, National Resource Centre for Dance. 1997

Sanders, L. Choreographer Fact Card: Richard Alston, National Resource Centre for Dance. 2002

Sanders, L. Choreographers Today: Henri Oguike. *Dancing Times*, March, 2003. pp.17-23

Schiavo, P. Saint Louis Symphony Programme Notes, www.slso.org/0304notes/10-18.htm, accessed 20/07/04. 2003

Steen, M. *The Lives and Times of the Great Composers*. Cambridge, Icon Books. 2003

Strachan, I., www.dschjournal.../.../rvs16op117.htm, accessed 05/08/04. 2002

Way, J. Sierra Chamber Society Program Notes, www.fuguemasters.com/dsch.html, accessed 05/08/04. 2002

Weitz, J. Program Notes: Ying Quartet/Cavani String Quartet, www.cmcolumbus.org, accessed 05/08/04. 2001